Matching Wits with the Million-Dollar Mind

MATCHING WITS WITH THE MILLION-DOLLAR MIND

The World's Hardest Trivia Quizzes from America's First Quiz Show Millionaire

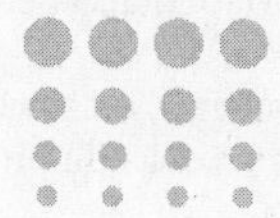

JOHN CARPENTER

with Rod L. Evans, PH.D.

BERKLEY BOOKS, NEW YORK

B
A Berkley Book
Published by The Berkley Publishing Group
A division of Penguin Putnam Inc.
375 Hudson Street
New York, New York 10014

Book design by Tiffany Kukec
Cover design and art by Dan Bond
Cover photograph of John Carpenter by Creative Studio, Inc.

PRINTING HISTORY
Berkley trade paperback edition / January 2002

Visit our website at
www.penguinputnam.com

Library of Congress Cataloging-in-Publication Data

Carpenter, John.
Matching wits with the million-dollar mind : the world's hardest trivia quizzes from America's first quiz show Millionaire / John Carpenter with Rod L. Evans.
p. cm.
ISBN 0-425-18319-X
1. Quiz shows. 2. Questions and answers. 3. Who wants to be a millionaire—Miscellanea.
I. Evans, Rod L., 1956– II. Title.

GV1507.Q5 C27 2002
031.02—dc21
2001052435

PRINTED IN THE UNITED STATES OF AMERICA

10 9 8 7 6 5 4 3 2 1

FOREWORD

The most popular TV quiz show since the 1950s, *Who Wants to Be a Millionaire,* began on August 16, 1999. Introduced in the summer rather than in the fall, broadcast in prime time on thirteen of fourteen consecutive nights, and designed to allow people outside help to answer questions, the show, based on a successful British program, broke many long-accepted rules of American television. Although Americans have loved TV game shows since their introduction in the fifties, *Who Wants to Be a Millionaire* has generated more interest and more excitement than all other quiz shows in the last several decades. People have been staging social gatherings for it and watching it in such places as bars and health clubs. In short, the show has been a hot topic of national discourse in all forms of media since it began. People can now play the game every day on the Internet and on a CD.

The most widely discussed episode of the show was that in which John Carpenter, an IRS agent, won a million dollars on November 18, 1999. His achievement was noteworthy not only because of the sum won but also because of the way in which he won it. With total self-confidence Carpenter *easily* answered all questions without any of the help permitted from others. For the million-dollar question Carpenter called his father, not to help him answer the question, but to inform him that Carpenter was going to win the million dollars. As *People* magazine put it, Carpenter answered the questions with "cold-blooded cyborg efficiency."

Carpenter's achievement made him an extraordinary celebrity, earning him a spot on not only *Live! with Regis and Kathy Lee* but also *Good Morning America, Entertainment Tonight,* the *Late Show with David Letterman,* and *Saturday Night Live.* What is more, it even landed his picture on the cover of *TV Guide* as well as *People* magazine, which presented a six-page article on him in the December 6, 1999 issue. In the year 2000, he was often on TV discussing what life has been like since he won the million dollars. In 2001, he appeared as a guest on several episodes of the critically acclaimed HBO drama *Oz.*

In his second appearance in the hot seat, broadcast on May 24 and 25, 2000, John earned another distinction. Competing against former champions, all of whom agreed to give half of their winnings to charity, John won $250,000, while the other million-dollar winners won only $1,000.

A Rutgers graduate who majored in economics, John, known for his extraordinarily wide knowledge, regularly finishes the *New York Times* crossword puzzle at lunch. He prides himself on his attention to detail, a quality much needed by an IRS agent. Because of his remarkable gift for trivia and the fame and fortune it has won him, he is well qualified to create the world's hardest trivia quizzes.

—Rod L. Evans, Ph.D.

Preface

This book consists of three groups of tests. First, there are twenty-five tests created by John Carpenter. Each test contains questions that are progressively difficult. The areas and disciplines covered are numerous and diverse, including TV, movies, music, literature, sports, current events, history, geography, vocabulary, and so on. Second, there are twenty-five tests created by author and college philosophy professor Dr. Rod Evans. Those tests were given to John Carpenter, who took them and whose score is revealed at the end of each test. Although John answered most of the questions correctly, he missed some of them, indicated by asterisks by the answers. If you see no asterisk by an answer, you can conclude that John answered the question correctly.

The third and final section of questions consists of "million-dollar questions." Covering numerous subjects and disciplines, those questions are usually as difficult as any questions on TV quiz shows or anywhere else and are often *more* difficult. If you can answer as many as a third of those questions—even while guessing—you are impressive. If you can answer more than a third, you are extraordinarily knowledgeable, a walking encyclopedia. It is, however, possible to be bright and knowledgeable and still miss most of the "million-dollar questions." We designed them to be almost impossibly difficult, so that readers could learn something new and often interesting, bizarre, or surprising. Those questions can be especially entertaining when they are given to large groups of people at parties or other social gatherings. We hope that you will have as much fun reading and answering the questions as we had writing them. Good luck!

ACKNOWLEDGMENTS

We want to thank our literary agent, Sheree Bykofsky, whose services and support have been deeply appreciated. We want to thank also Denise Silvestro and her staff at The Berkley Publishing Group for believing in this work. Further, we want to thank Robin Hudgins, Elaine Dawson, and John's wife, Debbie, for their excellent word processing and support. Finally, we want to thank all our friends who have encouraged us, not least Rod Evans's friends, Brad Funk, Allison Calderbank, Rob Stewart, and David Mayer.

JOHN CARPENTER'S 25 CHALLENGES

I have designed these questions both to challenge and to entertain you. They cover numerous subjects, from popular culture to vocabulary, and the answers, especially for the most difficult questions, will probably surprise you—even with this warning. The value given to each question is admittedly somewhat subjective, since people's experiences, knowledge of different fields, and areas of interest often vary enormously. Nonetheless, I think that you will enjoy these tests and especially enjoy springing them on your friends.

JOHN CARPENTER'S CHALLENGE

$100

1. Into which of the following substances could you push a thumbtack?

   A. Asphalt
   B. Cork
   C. Brick
   D. Granite

$200

2. What color are ripe strawberries?

   A. Red
   B. White
   C. Green
   D. Purple

$300

3. What cat food can cats ask for by name?

   A. 9 Lives
   B. Meow Mix
   C. Tender Vittles
   D. Cat Chow

$500

4. A decathlon has how many events?

   A. 5
   B. 7
   C. 10
   D. 20

$1,000

5. What is an apothecary?

   A. Druggist
   B. Geologist
   C. Astronomer
   D. Stamp collector

$2,000

6. What American holiday falls on the first Monday in September?

   A. Veteran's Day　　**B.** Flag Day
   C. Memorial Day　　**D.** Labor Day

$4,000

7. What is the name of Roz's daughter on the TV show *Frasier*?

   A. May　　**B.** Alice
   C. Agnes　　**D.** Sandra

$8,000

8. In the movie *Goldfinger*, what was Goldfinger's first name?

   A. Cupric　　**B.** Argent
   C. Auric　　**D.** Cedric

$16,000

9. In the movie *The Big Chill*, what is the name of the dead friend?

   A. Sam Webber　　**B.** Harold Cooper
   C. Gardner Barnes　　**D.** Alex Chambers

$32,000

10. In the 2000 movie *Miss Congeniality*, in what pageant does Sandra Bullock pose as a contestant?

    A. Miss America　　**B.** Miss USA
    C. Miss United States　　**D.** Miss World

$64,000

11. The Teapot Dome scandal took its name from what?

    A. FBI code name for the investigation　　**B.** The mountain involved
    C. Naval oil reserve　　**D.** Coal mine

$125,000

12. In the winter of 2000, what supermodel teamed with Palm to create a signature brand of a personal digital assistant?

    A. Claudia Schiffer **B.** Cindy Crawford
    C. Pauline Poriszkova **D.** Christy Brinkley

$250,000

13. What is a barramundi?

    A. Snake **B.** Fish
    C. Goblet **D.** Tree

$500,000

14. Where is the Blue Mosque?

    A. Jerusalem **B.** Mecca
    C. Istanbul **D.** Jeddah

$1,000,000

15. What is the capital of Lithuania?

    A. Riga **B.** Tblisi
    C. Talinn **D.** Vilnius

ANSWERS ◆ TO JOHN CARPENTER'S CHALLENGE #1

1. B. *Cork*
2. A. *Red*
3. B. *Meow Mix*
4. C. *10*
5. A. *Druggist*
6. D. *Labor Day*
7. B. *Alice*
8. C. *Auric*
9. D. *Alex Chambers*
10. C. *Miss United States*
11. C. *Naval oil reserve*
12. A. *Claudia Schiffer*
13. B. *Fish*
14. C. *Istanbul*
15. D. *Vilnius*

JOHN CARPENTER'S CHALLENGE 2

$100

1. "Good night and don't let the bed bugs" do what?

   A. Fight
   B. Bite
   C. Drive drunk
   D. Stay up too late

$200

2. Which people would be most likely found in a circus?

   A. Lawyers
   B. Politicians
   C. Tax collectors
   D. Clowns

$300

3. What are the first three digits of a complete phone number?

   A. Zip code
   B. Exchange
   C. Area code
   D. Address

$500

4. Where on your body would you wear a fedora?

   A. Feet
   B. Hands
   C. Over a shirt
   D. Head

$1,000

5. Which soft drink advertised that it had the taste of "lymon"?

   A. Sprite
   B. 7 Up
   C. Mountain Dew
   D. Fresca

$2,000

6. What are the cartoon characters Heckle and Jeckle?

A. Blackbirds **B.** Chipmunks
C. Kids **D.** Salesmen

$4,000

7. What shape is a dowel?

A. Pyramidal **B.** Cylindrical
C. Spherical **D.** Trapezoid

$8,000

8. What is a proboscis?

A. Tail **B.** Horn
C. Snout **D.** Stalk

$16,000

9. What do trenchermen do well?

A. Drink **B.** Dig
C. Smoke **D.** Eat

$32,000

10. The former lead singer of what band starred in the 2000 movie *Dancer in the Dark*?

A. Thompson Twins **B.** The Sugarcubes
C. A Flock of Seagulls **D.** ABC

$64,000

11. What shape is a ziggurat?

A. Pyramidal **B.** Spherical
C. Cube-shaped **D.** Obelisk-shaped

$125,000

12. Something that is coriaceous resembles what?

A. Trees | **B.** Rocks
C. Marble | **D.** Leather

$250,000

13. Who was pictured on the Great Seal of the Confederacy?

A. George Washington | **B.** Jefferson Davis
C. Thomas Jefferson | **D.** Robert E. Lee

$500,000

14. How many people serve on the Federal Reserve Bank's Board of Governors?

A. 24 | **B.** 12
C. 9 | **D.** 5

$1,000,000

15. Where was the easternmost terminus of the Oregon Trail?

A. St. Louis, Missouri | **B.** Independence, Missouri
C. Kansas City, Missouri | **D.** Chicago, Illinois

ANSWERS ◆ TO JOHN CARPENTER'S CHALLENGE #2

1. B. *Bite*
2. D. *Clowns*
3. C. *Area code*
4. D. *Head*
5. A. *Sprite*
6. A. *Blackbirds*
7. B. *Cylindrical*
8. C. *Snout*
9. D. *Eat*
10. B. *The Sugarcubes*
11. A. *Pyramidal*
12. D. *Leather*
13. A. *George Washington*
14. D. *5*
15. B. *Independence, Missouri*

JOHN CARPENTER'S CHALLENGE 3

$100

1. "SUV" stands for what?

   A. Sport Utility Vehicle
   B. Stick Up Vineyards
   C. Slow Up Vehicles
   D. Super Ugly Vehicle

$200

2. What does "hi-fi" stand for?

   A. High finance
   B. Historical fiction
   C. High fidelity
   D. Hit and finish

$300

3. Within the human body, where are the quads?

   A. Arms
   B. Neck
   C. Thighs
   D. Back

$500

4. What is a nom de plume?

   A. Alias
   B. Pen name
   C. Stage name
   D. Last name

$1,000

5. Which word doesn't mean "nothing"?

   A. Zilch
   B. Nada
   C. Schmaltz
   D. Nichts

$2,000

6. In what month would you most likely see a menorah?

A. December
B. January
C. October
D. August

$4,000

7. What is the name of Martha Stewart's magazine?

A. *Good Living*
B. *Good Things*
C. *Town and Country*
D. *Living*

$8,000

8. When does the U.S. Supreme Court begin its session?

A. New Year's Day
B. First Monday in October
C. Last Monday in August
D. Labor Day

$16,000

9. What is used in semaphore signaling?

A. Lights
B. Smoke
C. Flags
D. Knocking

$32,000

10. What color is sauternes wine?

A. Red
B. White
C. Golden
D. Rosé

$64,000

11. What was the name of the Allied invasion of Europe on June 6, 1944?

A. Operation Avalanche
B. Operation Sea Lion
C. Operation Overlord
D. Operation Crossroads

$125,000

12. Who was the first left-handed American president?

    A. John Tyler — **B.** James Polk
    C. Millard Fillmore — **D.** James Garfield

$250,000

13. What country's rebel group is called FARC?

    A. Angola — **B.** Peru
    C. Mexico — **D.** Colombia

$500,000

14. What name was on a sign over Winnie the Pooh's door?

    A. Eeyore — **B.** Saunders
    C. Milne — **D.** Smythe

$1,000,000

15. What Hindu god has the head of an elephant?

    A. Siva — **B.** Ganesha
    C. Brahma — **D.** Surya

ANSWERS ◆ TO JOHN CARPENTER'S CHALLENGE #3

1. A. *Sport Utility Vehicle*
2. C. *High fidelity*
3. C. *Thighs*
4. B. *Pen name*
5. C. *Schmaltz*
6. A. *December*
7. D. *Living*
8. B. *First Monday in October*
9. C. *Flags*
10. B. *White*
11. C. *Operation Overlord*
12. D. *James Garfield*
13. D. *Colombia*
14. B. *Saunders*
15. B. *Ganesha*

JOHN CARPENTER'S CHALLENGE 4

$100

1. In the nursery rhyme, "Simple Simon met a" what?

   A. Baker **B.** Fireman
   C. Candlestick maker **D.** Pieman

$200

2. To remove a splinter, you would most likely use what?

   A. Sandpaper **B.** Screwdriver
   C. Tweezers **D.** Scalpel

$300

3. What is a pirate flag commonly called?

   A. Jolly Roger **B.** Jolly Rancher
   C. Stars and Bars **D.** Mike and Ike

$500

4. What is a Geiger counter used to measure?

   A. Severity of earthquakes **B.** Speed of wind
   C. Radioactivity **D.** Density of gases

$1,000

5. In Spanish, what does *lobo* mean?

   A. Crazy **B.** Tall
   C. Young **D.** Wolf

$2,000

6. In the comic strip *Bloom County*, what was Opus?

A. Dog
B. Lawyer
C. Woodchuck
D. Penguin

$4,000

7. What is the practice called in which a merchant advertises one product and then pushes a different, more expensive product?

A. Clean and jerk
B. Attract and divert
C. Treat and trick
D. Bait and switch

$8,000

8. The effects of a nuclear attack on what city is shown in *The Day After*, a made-for-TV movie?

A. Lawrence, Kansas
B. Norman, Oklahoma
C. Camden, Maine
D. Columbus, Ohio

$16,000

9. On a bottle of Beck's beer, what object is on the shield in its logo?

A. Castle
B. Horse
C. Key
D. Harp

$32,000

10. How many members are in the U.S. House of Representatives?

A. 100
B. 235
C. 435
D. 535

$64,000

11. What brand of candy bar does George lose in a classic *Seinfeld* episode?

A. Twix
B. Kit Kat
C. Almond Joy
D. Mounds

$125,000

12. From what does George Eliot's *Middlemarch* take its name?

A. Mountain **B.** Town

C. Family name **D.** Time of year

$250,000

13. In Japan, what is a torii?

A. Arch **B.** Boat

C. Sumo wrestler's robe **D.** Cart

$500,000

14. Which of the following London landmarks was *not* designed by Sir Christopher Wren?

A. St. Paul's Cathedral **B.** Royal Exchange

C. St. Anne Lutheran Church **D.** Houses of Parliament

$1,000,000

15. What comic strip features characters with the same names as the creator's former coworkers at the Art Instruction School of America?

A. *Dilbert* **B.** *Family Circus*

C. *Peanuts* **D.** *Bloom County*

ANSWERS ◆ TO JOHN CARPENTER'S CHALLENGE #4

1. D. *Pieman*
2. C. *Tweezers*
3. A. *Jolly Roger*
4. C. *Radioactivity*
5. D. *Wolf*
6. D. *Penguin*
7. D. *Bait and switch*
8. A. *Lawrence, Kansas*
9. C. *Key*
10. C. 435
11. A. *Twix*
12. B. *Town*
13. A. *Arch*
14. D. *Houses of Parliament*
15. C. Peanuts

JOHN CARPENTER'S CHALLENGE 5

$100

1. What animal says "ribbit"?

   A. Frog
   B. Bear
   C. Rabbit
   D. Dog

$200

2. If you wanted to rid your home of a fly, what would be the best strategy?

   A. Buy a cat
   B. Get a flyswatter
   C. Call the cops
   D. Look for a stick of dynamite

$300

3. To prevent a dog from biting, you might put what over its mouth?

   A. Bandana
   B. Leash
   C. Muzzle
   D. Hand

$500

4. What piece of furniture is a La-Z-Boy?

   A. Table
   B. Chair
   C. Shelf
   D. Sink

$1,000

5. In what movie does Robert De Niro deliver the famous "You talking to me?" monologue?

   A. *The Godfather*
   B. *This Boy's Life*
   C. *Taxi Driver*
   D. *Goodfellas*

$2,000

6. According to Suze Orman, what should you have the courage to do?

   A. Grow up
   B. Be rich
   C. Pursue excellence
   D. Retire early

$4,000

7. According to the Bible, what was Jesus' first miracle?

   A. Feeding the multitudes
   B. Casting out demons
   C. Raising Lazarus from the dead
   D. Turning water into wine

$8,000

8. What NFL team in 2000 honored the memory of a former coach by putting a fedora-shaped patch on their uniforms?

   A. Green Bay Packers
   B. Dallas Cowboys
   C. Chicago Bears
   D. New York Giants

$16,000

9. In the movie *The Gods Must Be Crazy*, the appearance of what object in an African bushman's life causes an interesting course of events?

   A. Bible
   B. Box of matches
   C. Coke bottle
   D. Hula Hoop

$32,000

10. What does the Latin phrase *primus inter pares* mean?

    A. First born
    B. Evenly matched
    C. Long-lived
    D. First among equals

$64,000

11. Where in London is the newspaper district?

    A. Carnaby Street
    B. Fleet Street
    C. Whitechapel
    D. Southwark

$125,000

12. What are the dimensions of a cord of wood in feet?

A. 4x4x8
B. 10x10x10
C. 4x4x4
D. 1x6x3

$250,000

13. What type of wood are baseball bats made of?

A. Oak
B. Maple
C. Beech
D. Ash

$500,000

14. Where is the liquor called Geneva produced?

A. Switzerland
B. Italy
C. Netherlands
D. Portugal

$1,000,000

15. In what classic Broadway musical did angels do the Heaven Hop?

A. *Damn Yankees*
B. *Anything Goes*
C. *Guys and Dolls*
D. *Once Upon A Mattress*

ANSWERS ◆ TO JOHN CARPENTER'S CHALLENGE #5

1. A. *Frog*
2. B. *Get a flyswatter*
3. C. *Muzzle*
4. B. *Chair*
5. C. Taxi Driver
6. B. *Be rich*
7. D. *Turning water into wine*
8. B. *Dallas Cowboys*
9. C. Coke bottle
10. D. *First among equals*
11. B. *Fleet Street*
12. A. *4x4x8*
13. D. *Ash*
14. C. *Netherlands*
15. B. Anything Goes

JOHN CARPENTER'S CHALLENGE 6

$100

1. Which of the following items is *not* worn around the wrist?

A. Belt
B. Bracelet
C. Watch
D. Bangle

$200

2. What is the most expensive property in the original Monopoly game?

A. Pennsylvania Avenue
B. Free Parking
C. Boardwalk
D. Jail

$300

3. What was the name of the movie star on *Gilligan's Island*?

A. Ginger
B. Mrs. Howell
C. Mary Ann
D. Wilma

$500

4. What is a divan?

A. Table
B. Shelf
C. Sink
D. Couch

$1,000

5. Putting a horizontal line over a Roman numeral multiplies it by what?

A. 5
B. 10
C. 100
D. 1000

$2,000

6. In *Winnie the Pooh*, what sort of animal is Tigger?

A. Lion
B. Tiger
C. Leopard
D. Donkey

$4,000

7. In 2000, Heinz introduced ketchup in a newly shaped bottle and in what color?

A. Yellow
B. Blue
C. White
D. Green

$8,000

8. What color is the *O* in Mobil Oil's logo?

A. Blue
B. White
C. Red
D. Black

$16,000

9. What is the name of the missile submarine at the center of the movie *Crimson Tide*?

A. *Harvard*
B. *Red Hook*
C. *Gettysburg*
D. *Alabama*

$32,000

10. In what American city is the National D-Day Museum?

A. New York City, New York
B. New Orleans, Louisiana
C. Charleston, South Carolina
D. Washington, D.C.

$64,000

11. What artist is famous for "soft sculptures"?

A. Henry Moore
B. Claes Oldenburg
C. Jeff Koons
D. George Segal

$125,000

12. What modern city is designed to resemble a jet plane?

A. Brasilia | **B.** Canberra
C. Bonn | **D.** New Delhi

$250,000

13. What president threatened to outlaw football because of its violence?

A. Theodore Roosevelt | **B.** Woodrow Wilson
C. Franklin D. Roosevelt | **D.** William Howard Taft

$500,000

14. What gas is contained in a case used to preserve the original U.S. Constitution?

A. Krypton | **B.** Radon
C. Xenon | **D.** Argon

$1,000,000

15. What is a sabot made of?

A. Metal | **B.** Wood
C. Leather | **D.** Stone

ANSWERS ♦ TO JOHN CARPENTER'S CHALLENGE #6

1. A. *Belt*
2. C. *Boardwalk*
3. A. *Ginger*
4. D. *Couch*
5. D. *1000*
6. B. *Tiger*
7. D. *Green*
8. C. *Red*
9. D. *Alabama*
10. B. *New Orleans, Louisiana*
11. B. *Claes Oldenburg*
12. A. *Brasilia*
13. A. *Theodore Roosevelt*
14. D. *Argon*
15. B. *Wood*

JOHN CARPENTER'S CHALLENGE 7

$100

1. Which item would it be most useful to have if you fell out of a plane?

   A. Parachute
   B. Baseball cap
   C. Umbrella
   D. Anchor

$200

2. To lie in wait to attack is called what?

   A. Broadside
   B. Ambush
   C. Assault
   D. Battery

$300

3. What kind of energy does a dam help produce?

   A. Nuclear
   B. Solar
   C. Hydroelectric
   D. Kinetic

$500

4. What was the pen name of Samuel Clemens?

   A. Theodore Dreiser
   B. Bret Harte
   C. James Fenimore Cooper
   D. Mark Twain

$1,000

5. The First World War was touched off by the assassination of Archduke Franz Ferdinand of what country?

   A. Austria
   B. Serbia
   C. Hungary
   D. Germany

$2,000

6. On a standard touchtone phone, which word can be spelled using only the 4, 5, and 6 buttons?

A. Glam **B.** Igloo
C. Lope **D.** Fend

$4,000

7. What book was the follow-up to *The Tao of Pooh*?

A. *The Zen of Eeyor* **B.** *The Te of Piglet*
C. *Kanga's Rubiyat* **D.** *The Chakra of Christopher Robin*

$8,000

8. With what sport is Dick Vitale associated?

A. Swimming **B.** College football
C. Figure skating **D.** College basketball

$16,000

9. What is used to transmit sound to the brain?

A. Optic nerve **B.** Olfactory nerve
C. Otic nerve **D.** Eardrum

$32,000

10. What is the movie *Quicksilver* about?

A. Hockey players **B.** Chemists
C. Fighter pilots **D.** Bicycle messengers

$64,000

11. How does Ethan Frome try to kill himself?

A. Sledding **B.** Poisoning
C. Drowning **D.** Shooting himself

$125,000

12. Which one of the following people was born Florence Nightingale Graham?

    A. Clara Barton
    B. Elizabeth Arden
    C. Courtney Love
    D. Laura Ashley

$250,000

13. Which of the following stories features something resembling the mythical Scandinavian monster called the Kraken?

    A. *The Maelstrom*
    B. *The Pit and the Pendulum*
    C. *20,000 Leagues Under the Sea*
    D. *Frankenstein*

$500,000

14. Where in the human body will you find the xyphoid process?

    A. Pancreas
    B. Brain
    C. Heart
    D. Chest

$1,000,000

15. Who was described by an admirer as "mad, bad, and dangerous to know"?

    A. Edgar Allen Poe
    B. Lord Byron
    C. Ernest Hemingway
    D. Mozart

ANSWERS ◆ TO JOHN CARPENTER'S CHALLENGE #7

1. A. *Parachute*
2. B. *Ambush*
3. C. *Hydroelectric*
4. D. *Mark Twain*
5. A. *Austria*
6. B. *Igloo*
7. B. The Te of Piglet
8. D. *College basketball*
9. C. *Otic nerve*
10. D. *Bicycle messengers*
11. A. *Sledding*
12. B. *Elizabeth Arden*
13. C. 20,000 Leagues Under the Sea
14. D. *Chest*
15. B. *Lord Byron*

JOHN CARPENTER'S CHALLENGE

$100

1. If one is elated, one can be said to walk on what?

   A. Coals
   B. Air
   C. Water
   D. The wild side

$200

2. At the end of a party, an extremely drunken person might be wearing what?

   A. Tuxedo
   B. Name tag
   C. Smile
   D. Lampshade

$300

3. Performing without a script is to do what?

   A. *A capella*
   B. Method act
   C. Ad lib
   D. Scenery-chew

$500

4. What is the highest speed on most blenders?

   A. Chop
   B. Blend
   C. Liquefy
   D. Crush

$1,000

5. Vociferous people are what?

   A. Loud
   B. Hungry
   C. Smelly
   D. Excited

$2,000

6. What will you find inside a PEZ dispenser?

A. Gumballs
B. Motor oil
C. Candy
D. Hand lotion

$4,000

7. Where in the house would you most likely find andirons?

A. Sewing room
B. Kitchen
C. Greenhouse
D. Fireplace

$8,000

8. Which of the following describes television's Mr. Clean?

A. He is bald.
B. He has only one eye.
C. He is shirtless.
D. He has a nose ring.

$16,000

9. In what state does the 1998 Ang Lee movie *The Ice Storm* depict events over a weekend?

A. Minnesota
B. Connecticut
C. Vermont
D. New York

$32,000

10. *Monty Python's Flying Circus* episodes began with an old man uttering what word?

A. Help
B. The
C. Augh
D. It's

$64,000

11. In which movie did Clint Eastwood utter the much-imitated words "Make my day"?

A. *Dirty Harry*
B. *Magnum Force*
C. *The Enforcer*
D. *Sudden Impact*

$125,000

12. What is unique about the 1918 Curtis Jenny 24¢ stamp?

  A. It was the first mass-produced stamp.
  B. It was round.
  C. It showed an upside-down plane.
  D. It was triangular.

$250,000

13. Between what two bodies of water do the Caucasus Mountains stretch?

  A. Caspian and Black Sea
  B. Pacific Ocean and Caribbean Sea
  C. Mediterranean and Black Sea
  D. Caspian and Aral Sea

$500,000

14. In what island group is the Bikini Atoll found?

  A. Mariana Islands
  B. Marshall Islands
  C. Solomon Islands
  D. Micronesia

$1,000,000

15. A civil engineer named Gaspard Coriolis has a law of physics named after him explaining what?

  A. Solar eclipse's "diamond ring" effect
  B. Aurora borealis
  C. Bullet's downward trajectory over long distances
  D. Curve of a bowling ball when thrown correctly

ANSWERS ◆ TO JOHN CARPENTER'S CHALLENGE #8

1. B. *Air*
2. D. *Lampshade*
3. C. *Ad lib*
4. C. *Liquefy*
5. A. *Loud*
6. C. *Candy*
7. D. *Fireplace*
8. A. *He is bald.*
9. B. *Connecticut*
10. D. *It's*
11. D. Sudden Impact
12. C. *It showed an upside-down plane.*
13. A. *Caspian and Black Sea*
14. B. *Marshall Islands*
15. C. *Bullet's downward trajectory over long distances*

JOHN CARPENTER'S CHALLENGE 9

$100

1. To be dismissed from one's job is to be given "the old" what?

   A. Get up and go
   B. Heave-ho
   C. College try
   D. Granddad

$200

2. What is the best man at a wedding supposed to do?

   A. Toast the bride and groom
   B. The chicken dance
   C. Test the wedding cake
   D. Work the bar

$300

3. Of what family of instrument is the flute a member?

   A. Brass
   B. Percussion
   C. Woodwind
   D. Strings

$500

4. What is an expectorant supposed to make you do?

   A. Fall asleep
   B. Help conceive a child
   C. Stop bleeding
   D. Cough

$1,000

5. According to the nursery rhyme, what scared away Miss Muffett?

   A. Snake
   B. Wolf
   C. Spider
   D. The price of tuffets

$2,000

6. What event was known as "ten days that shook the world"?

A. Cuban missile crisis
B. Berlin airlift
C. Kennedy assassination
D. Fall of the Berlin Wall

$4,000

7. In football, what does a yellow flag indicate?

A. Touchdown
B. Time out
C. Penalty
D. End of game

$8,000

8. What part of the body is injured if the ACL is affected?

A. Knee
B. Elbow
C. Neck
D. Shoulder

$16,000

9. At what college was the movie *Animal House* filmed?

A. Dartmouth
B. University of Illinois
C. University of Oregon
D. Harvard

$32,000

10. In the movie *Speed*, where did Sandra Bullock's character go to college?

A. Arizona State University
B. USC
C. University of Arizona
D. UCLA

$64,000

11. Which of the following Florida keys is farthest north?

A. Key Colony Beach
B. Key Biscayne
C. Key West
D. Key Largo

$125,000

12. What Egyptian god had the head of a jackal?

A. Seti | **B.** Horus
C. Anubis | **D.** Isis

$250,000

13. Who said "Men seldom make passes at girls who wear glasses"?

A. Ogden Nash | **B.** Oscar Wilde
C. Groucho Marx | **D.** Dorothy Parker

$500,000

14. Who said "Taxes are what we pay for civilized society"?

A. Benjamin Franklin | **B.** Oliver Wendell Holmes
C. Franklin Delano Roosevelt | **D.** John Marshall

$1,000,000

15. Of the following, which state is sometimes called the Sunset State?

A. Arizona | **B.** Washington
C. Alaska | **D.** California

ANSWERS ◆ TO JOHN CARPENTER'S CHALLENGE #9

1. B. *Heave-ho*
2. A. *Toast the bride and groom*
3. C. *Woodwind*
4. D. *Cough*
5. C. *Spider*
6. A. *Cuban missile crisis*
7. C. *Penalty*
8. A. *Knee*
9. C. *University of Oregon*
10. C. *University of Arizona*
11. B. *Key Biscayne*
12. C. *Anubis*
13. D. *Dorothy Parker*
14. B. *Oliver Wendell Holmes*
15. A. *Arizona* (though Alaska is sometimes called The *Land of the Midnight Sun*)

JOHN CARPENTER'S CHALLENGE 10

$100

1. According to a popular saying, it takes two to do what?

   A. Ice skate
   B. Square dance
   C. Tango
   D. Blow your nose

$200

2. Which of the following creatures has a mane?

   A. Dog
   B. Fish
   C. Cat
   D. Horse

$300

3. Where is the Miss America pageant held?

   A. Atlantic City
   B. Las Vegas
   C. Miami
   D. Charleston

$500

4. In what sport is a shuttlecock used?

   A. Shuffleboard
   B. Curling
   C. Badminton
   D. Squash

$1,000

5. In the nursery rhyme, how many fiddlers did King Cole have?

   A. 24
   B. 7
   C. 5
   D. 3

$2,000

6. What comic strip featured a character called the Shmoo?

A. *Pogo*
B. *Li'l Abner*
C. *Blondie*
D. *Popeye*

$4,000

7. What is a sweater that buttons fully down the front called?

A. Henley
B. Poncho
C. V-neck
D. Cardigan

$8,000

8. For what college did Julius Erving (Dr. J) play basketball?

A. UCLA
B. Marquette
C. University of Massachusetts
D. University of North Carolina

$16,000

9. What is James Bond's military rank?

A. Lieutenant
B. Colonel
C. Commander
D. Seaman

$32,000

10. In 2000, who was the emperor of Japan?

A. Hirohito
B. Akhito
C. Takeshita
D. Mejii

$64,000

11. Odovacar was the last what?

A. Mongol leader
B. Russian czar
C. Mohican
D. Roman emperor

$125,000

12. What is the real name of the Looney Toons musical theme?

    A. "Here Come the Clowns"
    B. "Merrily We Roll Along"
    C. "The Merry-Go-Round Broke Down"
    D. "This Is It"

$250,000

13. Hell's Canyon borders Idaho and what other state?

    A. Oregon
    B. Washington
    C. Montana
    D. Wyoming

$500,000

14. What was the subject of the political scandal known as the XYZ Affair?

    A. Bribery
    B. Espionage
    C. Sex
    D. Embezzlement

$1,000,000

15. Which president was in office during the Gilded Age?

    A. William Henry Harrison
    B. Abraham Lincoln
    C. William Howard Taft
    D. Rutherford B. Hayes

ANSWERS ◆ TO JOHN CARPENTER'S CHALLENGE #10

1. C. *Tango*
2. D. *Horse*
3. A. *Atlantic City*
4. C. *Badminton*
5. D. *3*
6. B. *Li'l Abner*
7. D. *Cardigan*
8. C. *University of Massachusetts*
9. C. *Commander*
10. B. *Akihito*
11. D. *Roman emperor*
12. B. *"Merrily We Roll Along"*
13. A. *Oregon*
14. A. *Bribery*
15. D. *Rutherford B. Hayes*

JOHN CARPENTER'S CHALLENGE 11

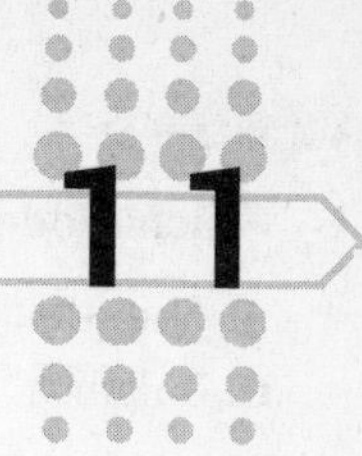

$100

1. For treating sore throats many people choose to gargle with what?

   A. Drano
   B. Salt water
   C. Dirty dishwater
   D. Battery acid

$200

2. What is a young goat called?

   A. Kid
   B. Nanny
   C. Colt
   D. Chip

$300

3. According to an advertisement, "it's not butter, it's" what?

   A. Dog food
   B. Peanut butter
   C. Parkay
   D. Better

$500

4. "PR" stands for public what?

   A. Reading
   B. Rest
   C. Relaxation
   D. Relations

$1,000

5. Flipper was a what?

   A. Shark
   B. Dog
   C. Seal
   D. Dolphin

$2,000

6. Which modern country contains the region of Transylvania?

   A. Romania **B.** Czech Republic
   C. Bulgaria **D.** Slovakia

$4,000

7. What is a gulag?

   A. Traditional Russian dance **B.** Tent
   C. Prison **D.** Stew

$8,000

8. What is the name of the hero of Maurice Sendak's *Where the Wild Things Are*?

   A. Max **B.** Mike
   C. Sam **D.** Ted

$16,000

9. What politician's nickname was the Kingfish?

   A. Huey Long **B.** Joe McCarthy
   C. Fiorello LaGuardia **D.** Theodore Roosevelt

$32,000

10. *Omerta* is a mafia term meaning what?

    A. Honor **B.** Respect
    C. Silence **D.** Revenge

$64,000

11. What are the Montgolfier brothers credited with inventing?

    A. Hot air balloon **B.** Wallpaper
    C. Indoor plumbing **D.** The French horn

$125,000

12. An EVA is more commonly known as what?

A. Orbit | **B.** Lift off
C. Spacewalk | **D.** Splashdown

$250,000

13. What did the most recently ratified U.S. Constitutional amendment address?

A. Voting age | **B.** Congressional pay
C. Abortion | **D.** Presidential vote for D.C.

$500,000

14. What is the term for someone from Barbados?

A. Barbadan | **B.** Barbudan
C. Bajan | **D.** Barban

$1,000,000

15. Which of the following creatures is haustellate?

A. Mosquito | **B.** Praying mantis
C. Tick | **D.** Caterpillar

ANSWERS ◆ TO JOHN CARPENTER'S CHALLENGE #11

1. B. *Salt water*
2. A. *Kid*
3. C. *Parkay*
4. D. *Relations*
5. D. *Dolphin*
6. A. *Romania*
7. C. *Prison*
8. A. *Max*
9. A. *Huey Long*
10. C. *Silence*
11. A. *Hot air balloon*
12. C. *Spacewalk ("EVA" means "extravehicular activity")*
13. B. *Congressional pay*
14. C. *Bajan*
15. A. *Mosquito (A haustellum is a tubular structure adapted for sucking blood or plant juices.)*

JOHN CARPENTER'S CHALLENGE 12

$100

1. Which prefix means "small"?

A. Maxi
B. Mini
C. Mono
D. Midi

$200

2. Who hunts "wabbits"?

A. Yosemite Sam
B. Sylvester
C. Elmer Fudd
D. Richard Wagner

$300

3. How many tentacles does an octopus have?

A. 8
B. 6
C. 5
D. 4

$500

4. What American folk hero died at the Alamo?

A. Daniel Boone
B. Sam Houston
C. Davy Crockett
D. John Henry

$1,000

5. If a quarterback passes the ball, and it is caught by a cornerback, what happened?

A. Fumble
B. Safety
C. Reception
D. Interception

$2,000

6. What is a maven?

A. Troublemaker
B. Religious person
C. Expert
D. Detective

$4,000

7. What animals helped Pavlov prove the phenomenon of conditioned response?

A. Hamsters
B. Dogs
C. Mice
D. Birds

$8,000

8. On what TV show was there a character named Maynard G. Krebs?

A. *Dobie Gillis*
B. *Mary Tyler Moore Show*
C. *Laugh-In*
D. *Soap*

$16,000

9. Rob Pilatus was a member of what eighties music group?

A. Romantics
B. Milli Vanilli
C. Modern English
D. UB40

$32,000

10. What member of Britain's royal family hosted the BBC documentary *Crown and Country*?

A. Prince Charles
B. Prince Edward
C. Queen Elizabeth
D. Princess Diana

$64,000

11. What architect's early works were called Prairie Houses?

A. Philip Johnson
B. Louis Sullivan
C. Frank Lloyd Wright
D. Ludwig Mies van der Rohe

$125,000

12. What is unusual about Charles Dickens's *Mystery of Edwin Drood*?

A. It is unfinished.
B. It contains no *Q*s.
C. It takes place in the U.S.
D. It is written in the first person.

$250,000

13. Which pitcher threw a pitch he called his "trouble ball"?

A. Dizzy Dean
B. Ferguson Jenkins
C. Satchel Paige
D. Cy Young

$500,000

14. Which poet said, "No bird soars too high, if he soars with his own wings"?

A. Blake
B. Shelley
C. Keats
D. Emerson

$1,000,000

15. What is the name of the international space station now under construction?

A. Peace
B. Next
C. One
D. Alpha

ANSWERS ◆ TO JOHN CARPENTER'S CHALLENGE #12

1. B. *Mini*
2. C. *Elmer Fudd*
3. A. 8
4. C. *Davy Crockett*
5. D. *Interception*
6. C. *Expert*
7. B. *Dogs*
8. A. Dobie Gillis
9. B. *Milli Vanilli*
10. B. *Prince Edward*
11. C. *Frank Lloyd Wright*
12. A. *It is unfinished.*
13. C. *Satchel Paige*
14. A. *Blake* (Proverbs of Hell)
15. D. *Alpha*

JOHN CARPENTER'S CHALLENGE 13

$100

1. What is a collection of maps called?

   A. Chronograph **B.** Catalog
   C. Atlas **D.** Astrolabe

$200

2. What bone is properly called the humerus?

   A. Wrist bone **B.** Kneecap
   C. Elbow **D.** Upper arm bone

$300

3. Which of the following is *not* a variety of apple?

   A. Granny Smith **B.** Bosc
   C. McIntosh **D.** Fuji

$500

4. In *Peanuts*, how much did Lucy originally charge for psychiatric help?

   A. One dollar **B.** A dime
   C. A nickel **D.** On a sliding scale

$1,000

5. In Yiddish, what is *kreplach*?

   A. Dumpling **B.** Sweet dessert
   C. Soup **D.** Fish

$2,000

6. How many teams compete in the Big Ten conference?

   A. 10 **B.** 11
   C. 12 **D.** 9

$4,000

7. In the Bible, who trades his birthright to his younger brother for food?

   A. Esau **B.** Jacob
   C. Cain **D.** Joshua

$8,000

8. In *Dune*, what is the name of the coveted hallucinogenic spice?

   A. Melange **B.** Ice-nine
   C. Oleander **D.** Sage

$16,000

9. How many four-year American colleges have names beginning with the letter *Z*?

   A. 1 **B.** 2
   C. 3 **D.** 0

$32,000

10. What South American leader sought asylum in England in 1999?

    A. Anastasio Somoza **B.** Juan Peron
    C. Augusto Pinochet **D.** Alberto Fujimori

$64,000

11. The Leopold-Loeb murder inspired what dramatic work?

    A. *The Most Dangerous Game* **B.** *Natural Born Killers*
    C. *The Haunting* **D.** *Rope*

$125,000

12. In 1998, what novel did the Modern Library name the best novel published in English of the century?

A. *Catch-22* **B.** *Ulysses*
C. *The Sound and the Fury* **D.** *The Great Gatsby*

$250,000

13. What is the last book in C. S. Lewis's *Narnia* series?

A. *The Lion, the Witch and the Wardrobe* **B.** *The Silver Chair*
C. *Prince Caspian* **D.** *The Last Battle*

$500,000

14. In what activity would you use a product known as OSB?

A. Surveying **B.** Home construction
C. Plumbing **D.** Cooking

$1,000,000

15. What word describes the skin of melanochroi?

A. Black **B.** Brown
C. Red **D.** Pale

ANSWERS ◆ TO JOHN CARPENTER'S CHALLENGE #13

1. C. *Atlas*
2. D. *Upper arm bone*
3. B. *Bosc (variety of pear)*
4. C. *A nickel*
5. A. *Dumpling*
6. B. *11*
7. A. Esau
8. A. *Melange*
9. D. *0*
10. C. *Augusto Pinochet*
11. D. Rope
12. B. Ulysses
13. D. The Last Battle
14. B. *Home construction (lumber)*
15. D. *Pale*

JOHN CARPENTER'S CHALLENGE 14

$100

1. As the saying goes, you should look before you what?

   A. Jump into a fire
   B. Eat Spam
   C. Observe
   D. Leap

$200

2. A bird in the hand is what?

   A. Messy
   B. Worth two in the bush
   C. Not in the cage
   D. Food for the cat

$300

3. From what creature does venison come?

   A. Moose
   B. Salmon
   C. Bear
   D. Deer

$500

4. What Yiddish word means a "gossipy woman"?

   A. *Schmutz*
   B. *Schlemiel*
   C. *Yentl*
   D. *Yenta*

$1,000

5. What company was famous for a series of rhyming roadside signs used for ads?

   A. Burma Shave
   B. Red Man Tobacco
   C. Chevrolet
   D. Esso

$2,000

6. In a 1970s ad campaign, what product is used to try to stop many things, including a speeding car?

   A. Peanut butter
   B. Shaving cream
   C. Superglue
   D. Cellophane tape

$4,000

7. Who was the voice of Charlie in the TV series *Charlie's Angels*?

   A. Ricardo Montalban
   B. Roger Moore
   C. John Forsythe
   D. Larry Hagman

$8,000

8. During what armed conflict does the Clint Eastwood movie *Heartbreak Ridge* take place?

   A. Persian Gulf War
   B. Falkland Island War
   C. Grenada Invasion
   D. Removal of Noriega

$16,000

9. Who makes the official announcement of the winner of the electoral college votes in the American presidential election?

   A. Current president
   B. House speaker
   C. Vice president
   D. Senate majority leader

$32,000

10. Which South American country does *not* contain any part of the Andes mountains?

    A. Chile
    B. Argentina
    C. Venezuela
    D. Uruguay

$64,000

11. Who is the subject of Bob Woodward's 2000 book *Maestro*?

    A. Bill Clinton
    B. Richard Nixon
    C. Leonard Bernstein
    D. Alan Greenspan

$125,000

12. In the 1970s which country's government banned Coca-Cola because the soft drink company refused to reveal its secret formula?

A. India　　**B.** Albania
C. China　　**D.** North Korea

$250,000

13. In what American city were the first ESPN X Games held?

A. Providence, Rhode Island　　**B.** Baltimore, Maryland
C. San Diego, California　　**D.** Denver, Colorado

$500,000

14. What band's name was taken from a Monty Python routine?

A. Gin Blossoms　　**B.** Toad the Wet Sprocket
C. Third Eye Blind　　**D.** Green Day

$1,000,000

15. Kwashiorkor is a disease resulting from a deficiency of what?

A. Protein　　**B.** Vitamin B_{12}
C. Dietary fiber　　**D.** Vitamin K

ANSWERS ◆ TO JOHN CARPENTER'S CHALLENGE #14

1. D. *Leap*
2. B. *Worth two in the bush*
3. D. *Deer*
4. D. *Yenta*
5. A. *Burma Shave*
6. B. *Shaving cream*
7. C. *John Forsythe*
8. C. *Grenada Invasion*
9. C. *Vice president*
10. D. *Uruguay*
11. D. *Alan Greenspan*
12. A. *India*
13. A. *Providence, Rhode Island*
14. B. *Toad the Wet Sprocket*
15. A. *Protein*

JOHN CARPENTER'S CHALLENGE 15

$100

1. If you're involved in an arrangement with others under which you share driving duties and expenses, you are involved in a what?

   A. Car pool **B.** Carbuncle
   C. Carboy **D.** Taxi business

$200

2. If a lawyer works pro bono, he works for what?

   A. His father **B.** Experience
   C. Cher **D.** No charge

$300

3. What drink is most closely associated with James Bond?

   A. Shirley Temple **B.** Vodka martini
   C. Zombie **D.** Screwdriver

$500

4. In what year was the first moon landing?

   A. 1963 **B.** 1969
   C. 1973 **D.** 1977

$1,000

5. In what country is Minsk?

   A. Belarus **B.** Ukraine
   C. Russia **D.** Georgia

$2,000

6. What are mukluks?

A. Boots
B. Mittens
C. Shelters
D. Eskimo fishing poles

$4,000

7. What is the name for a scarf made of fur?

A. Stole
B. Necktie
C. Boa
D. Bolo

$8,000

8. Everlast was the lead singer of what group?

A. Living Colour
B. Beastie Boys
C. Motley Crue
D. House of Pain

$16,000

9. With what holiday is the German city Obergammerau traditionally associated?

A. Christmas
B. Oktoberfest
C. Fasching
D. Easter

$32,000

10. Where did Diane in *Cheers* attend classes?

A. MIT
B. Boston University
C. Harvard
D. Tufts

$64,000

11. In what county is the pottery style majolica made?

A. Spain
B. Mexico
C. Portugal
D. Italy

$125,000

12. What rap group has a member whose stage name is his favorite food spelled backwards?

A. De La Soul | **B.** NWA
C. Beastie Boys | **D.** 2 Live Crew

$250,000

13. What country's flag is a mirror image of Ireland's?

A. Ivory Coast | **B.** Hungary
C. Italy | **D.** Costa Rica

$500,000

14. How did Alexander Graham Bell propose for people to answer the telephone?

A. "Greetings!" | **B.** "Ahoy"
C. "Received" | **D.** "Hello"

$1,000,000

15. Which country can be reached by phone from the U.S. without dialing a country code?

A. Grenada | **B.** Aruba
C. Belize | **D.** Cuba

ANSWERS ◆ TO JOHN CARPENTER'S CHALLENGE #15

1. A. *Car pool*
2. D. *No charge*
3. B. *Vodka martini*
4. B. *1969*
5. A. Belarus
6. A. *Boots*
7. C. *Boa*
8. D. *House of Pain*
9. A. *Christmas*
10. B. *Boston University*
11. D. *Italy*
12. A. *De La Soul (Trugoy/Yogurt)*
13. A. *Ivory Coast*
14. B. *"Ahoy"*
15. A. *Grenada*

JOHN CARPENTER'S CHALLENGE 16

$100

1. If you change the channel without getting off the couch, what did you probably use?

A. Psychokinesis **B.** Child
C. Satellite **D.** Remote control

$200

2. According to a popular saying, if it ain't broke, don't what?

A. Break it **B.** Fix it
C. Sell it **D.** Give it away

$300

3. An article of clothing that can be worn with either side showing is called what?

A. Reversible **B.** Threadbare
C. Convertible **D.** Hand-me-down

$500

4. What color is the body of the rooster on the box of Kellogg's Corn Flakes?

A. Red **B.** Green
C. Yellow **D.** White

$1,000

5. What is the favorite beer in *The Simpsons*?

A. Duff **B.** Fuzz
C. Fudd **D.** Bluff

$2,000

6. What is the service area between the kitchen and the dining room sometimes called?

A. Dumbwaiter
B. Butler's pantry
C. Mudroom
D. Wet bar

$4,000

7. In *Dharma and Greg,* what instrument does Dharma play?

A. Guitar
B. Accordion
C. Drums
D. Piano

$8,000

8. In the 2000 movie *Dogma,* who plays the role of God?

A. Matt Damon
B. Chris Rock
C. Silent Bob
D. Alanis Morisette

$16,000

9. Who was George Washington's secretary of state?

A. Alexander Hamilton
B. Thomas Jefferson
C. James Madison
D. John Adams

$32,000

10. What country is the Magyar Republic?

A. Malaysia
B. Greece
C. Hungary
D. Yugoslavia

$64,000

11. What government agency was headed by Marvin Runyon?

A. Post Office
B. CIA
C. Library of Congress
D. FBI

$125,000

12. What country was the first to celebrate the year 2000?

A. Nauru | **B.** Kiribati
C. Solomon Islands | **D.** New Guinea

$250,000

13. Which state name is *not* derived from a North American Indian word?

A. Kentucky | **B.** Mississippi
C. Delaware | **D.** Utah

$500,000

14. Where was actress Vivien Leigh born?

A. Wales | **B.** England
C. India | **D.** U.S.A.

$1,000,000

15. What U.S. president declared Thanksgiving to be on the fourth Thursday of November?

A. Abraham Lincoln | **B.** Theodore Roosevelt
C. Woodrow Wilson | **D.** Franklin D. Roosevelt

ANSWERS ◆ TO JOHN CARPENTER'S CHALLENGE #16

1. D. *Remote control*
2. B. *Fix it*
3. A. *Reversible*
4. B. *Green*
5. A. *Duff*
6. B. *Butler's pantry*
7. C. *Drums*
8. D. *Alanis Morisette*
9. B. *Thomas Jefferson*
10. C. *Hungary*
11. A. *Post Office*
12. B. *Kiribati*
13. C. *Delaware*
14. C. *India*
15. D. *Franklin D. Roosevelt*

JOHN CARPENTER'S CHALLENGE 17

$100

1. What words are you most likely to hear at a grocery store checkout?

   A. "Coffee or tea?"
   B. "Paper or plastic?"
   C. "Sink or swim?"
   D. "Smoking or nonsmoking?"

$200

2. Someone who just kicked the bucket did what?

   A. Recently died
   B. Expressed anger
   C. Played a child's game
   D. Got married

$300

3. What is a novice at something called?

   A. Yellow dog
   B. Blue moon
   C. Red herring
   D. Greenhorn

$500

4. The substance neoprene is most likely used to make what?

   A. Flippers
   B. Baseball glove
   C. Basketball backboard
   D. Wet suit

$1,000

5. About how many people live in the U.S.?

   A. A billion
   B. 280 million
   C. 80 million
   D. 28 million

$2,000

6. To what political party did George Washington belong?

A. Federalist | **B.** Republican
C. Whig | **D.** Democrat-Republican

$4,000

7. What American sitcom was inspired by the British series *Man About the House*?

A. *Seinfeld* | **B.** *Benson*
C. *Three's Company* | **D.** *Love, Sidney*

$8,000

8. What is the current name of the country in which Zoroastrianism originated?

A. Turkey | **B.** Iraq
C. Iran | **D.** Saudi Arabia

$16,000

9. If one is cyanotic, one has what?

A. Trouble breathing | **B.** Irregular heartbeat
C. Clammy skin | **D.** Blue skin

$32,000

10. What was the name of William Randolph Hearst's mansion in California?

A. Xanadu | **B.** The Hermitage
C. San Simeon | **D.** Cliffside

$64,000

11. With what NFL team did George Plimpton pose as a player and then write a book about his experiences?

A. Detroit Lions | **B.** Cincinnati Bengals
C. New York Giants | **D.** Chicago Bears

$125,000

12. What is a group of crows called?

A. Flock | **B.** Murder
C. Cloak | **D.** Crash

$250,000

13. In Greek mythology, who slew the Caledonian boar?

A. Hercules | **B.** Jason
C. Meleager | **D.** Achilles

$500,000

14. What company gave away the technology that later became the computer mouse?

A. Xerox | **B.** Microsoft
C. IBM | **D.** Hewlett-Packard

$1,000,000

15. What is the capital of Azerbaijan?

A. Talinn | **B.** Tblisi
C. Baku | **D.** Gäncä

ANSWERS ◆ TO JOHN CARPENTER'S CHALLENGE #17

1. B. *"Paper or plastic?"*
2. A. *Recently died*
3. D. *Greenhorn*
4. D. *Wet suit*
5. B. *280 million*
6. A. *Federalist*
7. C. Three's Company
8. C. *Iran*
9. D. *Blue skin*
10. C. *San Simeon*
11. A. *Detroit Lions*
12. B. *Murder*
13. C. *Meleager*
14. A. *Xerox*
15. C. *Baku*

JOHN CARPENTER'S CHALLENGE 18

$100

1. To balance your checkbook, which item would be most useful?

   A. Balance beam **B.** Two sawhorses
   C. A scale **D.** Calculator

$200

2. What did the extraterrestrial character in the movie *E. T.* repeatedly describe as his desire?

   A. Open a bank account **B.** Get a haircut
   C. Phone home **D.** Eat lox and bagels

$300

3. What does the word *sayonara* mean?

   A. Good-bye **B.** Hello
   C. Peace **D.** Greetings

$500

4. What is the capital of Texas?

   A. Amarillo **B.** Austin
   C. San Antonio **D.** Galveston

$1,000

5. How many items are in a gross?

   A. 100 **B.** 144
   C. 10,000 **D.** 150

$2,000

6. The word *carnival* comes from a Latin word for what?

A. Spring
B. Flesh
C. Feast
D. Dance

$4,000

7. What is the name of the fictional resort town in *Jaws*?

A. Amityville
B. Provinceville
C. Amity Island
D. Havenbrook

$8,000

8. What is the name of the country at war in the Marx Brothers movie *Duck Soup*?

A. Caledon
B. Marxiana
C. New Germania
D. Fredonia

$16,000

9. Who played opposite William Holden in *Sunset Boulevard*?

A. Gloria Swanson
B. Joan Crawford
C. Gloria Vanderbilt
D. Bette Davis

$32,000

10. Which sport debuted at the 2000 Sydney Olympics?

A. Softball
B. Beach volleyball
C. Women's pole vault
D. Rhythmic gymnastics

$64,000

11. Which island is one of the Lesser Antilles?

A. Cuba
B. Jamaica
C. Puerto Rico
D. Barbados

$125,000

12. What comic strip debuted in the *St. Paul Pioneer Press* as *Li'l Folks*?

A. *Bloom County* **B.** *Nancy*
C. *Peanuts* **D.** *Family Circus*

$250,000

13. The movie *The Krays* starred two brothers from what new wave band?

A. Spandau Ballet **B.** Thompson Twins
C. Duran Duran **D.** Plasmatics

$500,000

14. In what battle did David Farragut utter the famous words "Damn the torpedoes—full steam ahead!"?

A. Battle of Lake Erie **B.** Battle of the Chesapeake
C. Leyte Gulf **D.** Battle for New Orleans

$1,000,000

15. What expression was originally a nickname of Englishman Ambrose Philips?

A. Milquetoast **B.** Namby-Pamby
C. Airy-fairy **D.** Wishy-Washy

ANSWERS ◆ TO JOHN CARPENTER'S CHALLENGE #18

1. D. *Calculator*
2. C. *Phone home*
3. A. *Good-bye*
4. B. *Austin*
5. B. *144*
6. B. *Flesh*
7. C. *Amity Island*
8. D. *Fredonia*
9. A. *Gloria Swanson*
10. C. *Women's pole vault*
11. D. *Barbados*
12. C. Peanuts
13. A. *Spandau Ballet*
14. D. *Battle for New Orleans*
15. B. *Namby-Pamby*

JOHN CARPENTER'S CHALLENGE 19

$100

1. By definition, how many speak during a monologue?

   A. One
   B. Two
   C. None
   D. One too many

$200

2. If you have a yen for something, you what?

   A. Hate it
   B. Fear it
   C. Desire it
   D. Smoke it

$300

3. Where does a popular song tell you to "get your kicks"?

   A. Oregon Trail
   B. Route 61
   C. I-95
   D. Route 66

$500

4. What is the name for an organized activity in which two political candidates espouse their views head-to-head?

   A. Debate
   B. Interview
   C. Stump speech
   D. Chaos

$1,000

5. In the TV show *Frasier*, what is Niles, Frasier Crane's brother?

   A. Police officer
   B. Architect
   C. Psychiatrist
   D. Actor

$2,000

6. Who is the voice of the Grinch in the animated classic *How the Grinch Stole Christmas*?

A. Boris Karloff **B.** Vincent Price
C. Edward G. Robinson **D.** Lon Chaney, Jr.

$4,000

7. What is chateaubriand?

A. Island **B.** Steak
C. House **D.** Clothing

$8,000

8. What is a pattern pressed into paper to prevent forgery called?

A. Watermark **B.** Code
C. Perforation **D.** Signature

$16,000

9. What author wrote about Yoknapatawpha County?

A. Mark Twain **B.** John Steinbeck
C. William Faulkner **D.** Bret Harte

$32,000

10. Which Canadian province touches the most American states?

A. Alberta **B.** Saskatchewan
C. Ontario **D.** New Brunswick

$64,000

11. What country experienced the Velvet Revolution?

A. Czechoslovakia **B.** Romania
C. Poland **D.** Spain

$125,000

12. When did Australia issue its first stamp?

A. 1900 **B.** 1913
C. 1812 **D.** 1700

$250,000

13. The musician Bela Fleck is a virtuoso on what instrument?

A. Piano **B.** Accordion
C. Xylophone **D.** Banjo

$500,000

14. What is a baobab?

A. Tree **B.** Boat
C. Watering hole **D.** Rodent

$1,000,000

15. The word *myriad* literally refers to what specific number?

A. 100 **B.** 100,000
C. 1,000,000 **D.** 10,000

ANSWERS ◆ TO JOHN CARPENTER'S CHALLENGE #19

1. A. *One*
2. C. *Desire it*
3. D. *Route 66*
4. A. *Debate*
5. C. *Psychiatrist*
6. A. *Boris Karloff*
7. B. *Steak*
8. A. *Watermark*
9. C. *William Faulkner*
10. C. *Ontario*
11. A. *Czechoslovakia*
12. B. *1913*
13. D. *Banjo*
14. A. *Tree*
15. D. *10,000*

JOHN CARPENTER'S CHALLENGE 20

$100

1. To blend with his surroundings, a hunter would wear what?

A. Feather boa
B. Camouflage
C. Sequins
D. Bright orange

$200

2. If you are ambulatory, you have the ability to do what?

A. Fly
B. Swim
C. Drive an ambulance
D. Walk

$300

3. In what is sound measured?

A. Decibels
B. Machs
C. Lumens
D. Karats

$500

4. What is the right side of a ship called?

A. Bow
B. Starboard
C. Stern
D. Port

$1,000

5. What is the expression to describe a merchant with both stores and an online presence?

A. Clicks and mortar
B. On and off
C. Clicks and bricks
D. Bricks and mortar

$2,000

6. What is another name for the disease hydrophobia?

   A. Mumps **B.** Leprosy
   C. Rabies **D.** Arteriosclerosis

$4,000

7. What is the tarsus more commonly called?

   A. Wrist **B.** Elbow
   C. Breastbone **D.** Ankle

$8,000

8. The movie *The Taking of Pelham One Two Three* is about the hijacking of what?

   A. Cruise ship **B.** Subway
   C. Airplane **D.** Bus

$16,000

9. What country controls the Galapagos Islands?

   A. Peru **B.** Portugal
   C. Argentina **D.** Ecuador

$32,000

10. How many shots are in a jigger?

    A. 1.5 **B.** .5
    C. 2 **D.** 5

$64,000

11. What activity uses a Gunter's chain?

    A. Plumbing **B.** Surgery
    C. Surveying **D.** Cooking

$125,000

12. Between what two cities was the first transcontinental telephone demonstration?

A. New York and San Diego **B.** New York and San Francisco
C. Baltimore and San Francisco **D.** Philadelphia and San Diego

$250,000

13. Which Cole Porter musical features the song "Under My Skin"?

A. *The Gay Divorcee* **B.** *Anything Goes*
C. *Kiss Me Kate* **D.** *Red, Hot and Blue*

$500,000

14. In which year did England return Hong Kong to Chinese control?

A. 1996 **B.** 1997
C. 1998 **D.** 1999

$1,000,000

15. In what state are the Boston Mountains?

A. Washington **B.** Alaska
C. Arkansas **D.** Maine

ANSWERS ◆ TO JOHN CARPENTER'S CHALLENGE #20

1. B. *Camouflage*
2. D. *Walk*
3. A. *Decibels*
4. B. *Starboard*
5. C. *Clicks and bricks*
6. C. *Rabies*
7. D. *Ankle*
8. B. *Subway*
9. D. *Ecuador*
10. A. *1.5*
11. C. *Surveying*
12. B. *New York and San Francisco*
13. A. The Gay Divorcee
14. B. *1997*
15. C. *Arkansas*

JOHN CARPENTER'S CHALLENGE 21

$100

1. With what form of entertainment was Alfred Hitchcock most closely associated?

   A. Baseball
   B. Movies
   C. Video games
   D. Radio talk shows

$200

2. What state's capital is Sacramento?

   A. Massachusetts
   B. Pennsylvania
   C. California
   D. Virginia

$300

3. What is the name of President George W. Bush's wife?

   A. Laura
   B. Tipper
   C. Hillary
   D. Nancy

$500

4. Which state has the most electoral votes?

   A. New York
   B. Florida
   C. Texas
   D. California

$1,000

5. Almost all refrigerators are white or what other color?

   A. Yellow
   B. Red
   C. Almond
   D. Black

$2,000

6. What law school was supposed to be the setting for the movie *The Paper Chase*?

   A. Yale | **B.** Stanford
   C. Columbia | **D.** Harvard

$4,000

7. *Agoraphobia* comes from a Greek word for what?

   A. Basket | **B.** Market
   C. Sky | **D.** Wall

$8,000

8. For what famous ballerina did Aaron Copland write *Appalachian Spring*?

   A. Martha Graham | **B.** Anna Pavlova
   C. Agnes DeMille | **D.** Isadora Duncan

$16,000

9. What is the correct name of the symbol for "at" on the World Wide Web (WWW)?

   A. Amphora | **B.** Almon
   C. Carat | **D.** Ampersand

$32,000

10. Which country is *not* a member of OPEC?

   A. Venezuela | **B.** Nigeria
   C. Colombia | **D.** Indonesia

$64,000

11. Which country did *not* attack Israel in the Yom Kippur War?

   A. Egypt | **B.** Iraq
   C. Syria | **D.** Saudi Arabia

$125,000

12. What Major League Baseball team held a Disco Demolition Night after a game?

A. Chicago White Sox
B. New York Mets
C. Boston Red Sox
D. New York Yankees

$250,000

13. What state is called the Treasure State?

A. Idaho
B. Nevada
C. Montana
D. New Mexico

$500,000

14. From a character in what comic strip did the Jeep get its name?

A. *Li'l Abner*
B. *Popeye*
C. *Pogo*
D. *The Katzenjammer Kids*

$1,000,000

15. Who are the figures depicted in Grant Wood's painting *American Gothic*?

A. His mother and father
B. His sister and dentist
C. Neighbors
D. Aunt and milkman

ANSWERS ◆ TO JOHN CARPENTER'S CHALLENGE #21

1. B. *Movies*
2. C. *California*
3. A. *Laura*
4. D. *California*
5. C. Almond
6. D. *Harvard*
7. B. *Market*
8. A. *Martha Graham*
9. A. *Amphora*
10. C. *Colombia*
11. D. *Saudi Arabia*
12. A. *Chicago White Sox*
13. C. *Montana*
14. B. Popeye
15. B. *His sister and dentist*

JOHN CARPENTER'S CHALLENGE 22

$100

1. A decision made without thinking is called what?

   A. Knee-jerk　　**B.** Hair-pull
   C. Head-slap　　**D.** Congressional action

$200

2. In a series of advertisements, Sprint claims you can hear what clearly?

   A. A doorbell ring　　**B.** Your mother call
   C. A pin drop　　**D.** Gunshots

$300

3. How long is a U.S. senator's term of office?

   A. 2 years　　**B.** 4 years
   C. 6 years　　**D.** Life

$500

4. Advertisements for what armed force featured a man fighting a dragon?

   A. Army　　**B.** Air Force
   C. Navy　　**D.** Marines

$1,000

5. What country has the most nuclear plants?

   A. Japan　　**B.** United States
   C. France　　**D.** Russia

$2,000

6. Which of the following is an inert gas?

A. Radon | **B.** Hydrogen
C. Oxygen | **D.** Nitrogen

$4,000

7. In the 1998 movie *There's Something About Mary*, what NFL player makes a surprise appearance in the end?

A. Deion Sanders | **B.** Brett Favre
C. Jerry Rice | **D.** Steve Young

$8,000

8. What is the literal meaning of the word *philosophy*?

A. Love of knowledge | **B.** Love of truth
C. Love of thought | **D.** Love of wisdom

$16,000

9. Which company's ad campaign in the early nineties featured a character called the Noid?

A. Pizza Hut | **B.** Nike
C. Domino's Pizza | **D.** Kodak

$32,000

10. What is the adjective meaning "related to George Bernard Shaw"?

A. Georgian | **B.** Shavian
C. Shawistic | **D.** Shawian

$64,000

11. In September 2000, what was the first college football program to amass 800 wins?

A. Yale | **B.** Rutgers
C. University of Michigan | **D.** Harvard

$125,000

12. Who won the first World Cup of Soccer?

A. Argentina **B.** United States
C. Brazil **D.** Uruguay

$250,000

13. The former leader of what new wave band is the composer of the theme to *The Simpsons*?

A. ABC **B.** Oingo Boingo
C. Rockwell **D.** Talking Heads

$500,000

14. Astronaut David Wolf was the first to do what in outer space?

A. Get married **B.** Quote from Shakespeare
C. Belch **D.** Vote

$1,000,000

15. Who was the last man to set foot on the moon?

A. Pete Conrad **B.** Harrison H. Schmitt
C. Alan Shepard **D.** Scott Carpenter

ANSWERS ◆ TO JOHN CARPENTER'S CHALLENGE #22

1. A. *Knee-jerk*
2. C. *A pin drop*
3. C. *6 years*
4. D. *Marines*
5. B. *United States*
6. A. *Radon*
7. B. *Brett Favre*
8. D. *Love of wisdom*
9. C. *Domino's Pizza*
10. B. *Shavian*
11. A. *Yale*
12. D. *Uruguay*
13. B. *Oingo Boingo*
14. D. *Vote*
15. B. *Harrison H. Schmitt*

JOHN CARPENTER'S CHALLENGE 23

$100

1. Folk wisdom has it that pets resemble what?

   A. Their food
   B. Their owners
   C. Abraham Lincoln
   D. Their sleeping places

$200

2. What is a young cat called?

   A. Tom
   B. Whelp
   C. Kitten
   D. Foal

$300

3. In what month do Americans vote for a president?

   A. February
   B. March
   C. April
   D. November

$500

4. "Isn't that special?" was said by which character on *Saturday Night Live*?

   A. The Church Lady
   B. Franz
   C. Hans
   D. Velvet Jones

$1,000

5. Cerulean is a shade of what?

   A. Purple
   B. Green
   C. Yellow
   D. Blue

$2,000

6. What magical substance, found on Paradise Island, was molded into golden belts and bracelets and gave Wonder Woman her superpower?

   A. Feminum | **B.** Virilium
   C. Amazonium | **D.** Encomium

$4,000

7. What Woody Allen movie takes its title from a book by David Reubens?

   A. *Sleeper* | **B.** *Everything You Wanted to Know About Sex*
   C. *Take The Money And Run* | **D.** *Bananas*

$8,000

8. Who created the fictional detective Miss Jane Marple?

   A. Ellery Queen | **B.** Dorothy Sayers
   C. Agatha Christie | **D.** A.A. Fair

$16,000

9. Who was the subject of the movie *Somebody Up There Likes Me*?

   A. Lou Gehrig | **B.** Rocky Marciano
   C. Audie Murphy | **D.** Rocky Graziano

$32,000

10. For what high-tech company did the post-modern performance group Blue Man Group appear in advertisements in 2000?

    A. Microsoft | **B.** Cisco
    C. Nortel | **D.** Intel

$64,000

11. What is Upper Volta now called?

    A. Zimbabwe | **B.** Burkina Faso
    C. Sudan | **D.** Congo

$125,000

12. At what college did the Talking Heads meet?

A. MIT
B. Rhode Island School of Design
C. University of Michigan
D. Brown University

$250,000

13. The Strait of Juan de Fuca divides what two countries?

A. U.S. and Canada
B. Cuba and Jamaica
C. Cuba and the U.S.
D. Spain and Morocco

$500,000

14. Whose hand "played" the character of Thing on the TV show *The Addams Family*?

A. John Astin (Gomez Addams)
B. Jackie Coogan (Uncle Fester)
C. Ken Weatherwax (Pugsley Addams)
D. Ted Cassidy (Lurch)

$1,000,000

15. What hip-hop group features a member whose father is an award-winning playwright?

A. Public Enemy
B. Arrested Development
C. Beastie Boys
D. Wu Tang Clan

ANSWERS ◆ TO JOHN CARPENTER'S CHALLENGE #23

1. B. *Their owners*
2. C. *Kitten*
3. D. *November*
4. A. *The Church Lady*
5. D. *Blue*
6. A. *Feminum*
7. B. Everything You Wanted to Know About Sex
8. C. *Agatha Christie*
9. D. *Rocky Graziano*
10. D. *Intel*
11. B. *Burkina Faso*
12. B. *Rhode Island School of Design*
13. A. *U.S. and Canada*
14. D. *Ted Cassidy (Lurch)*
15. C. *Beastie Boys*

JOHN CARPENTER'S CHALLENGE 24

$100

1. Where would you look for the meaning of a word?

   A. Menu
   B. Atlas
   C. Phone book
   D. Dictionary

$200

2. What is added to swimming pools?

   A. Kool-Aid
   B. Alka-Seltzer
   C. Chlorine
   D. Powdered water

$300

3. How many doors does a coupe have?

   A. 2
   B. 3
   C. 4
   D. None

$500

4. What does an antibiotic attack?

   A. Phagocytes
   B. Bacteria
   C. Bile
   D. Viruses

$1,000

5. What is the Social Security tax also called?

   A. FUTA
   B. SSI
   C. Headstart
   D. FICA

$2,000

6. Who originally theorized about the id, ego, and superego?

A. Jung | **B.** Freud
C. Skinner | **D.** Adler

$4,000

7. By what name is the naturalist Steve Irwin better known?

A. The Crocodile Hunter | **B.** Doctor Doolittle
C. Mr. Wizard | **D.** Mr. Lizard

$8,000

8. What color are Japanese maple leaves?

A. Green | **B.** Red
C. White | **D.** Yellow

$16,000

9. Which of the following Robert De Niro movies does *not* contain Joe Pesci?

A. *Guilty by Suspicion* | **B.** *Raging Bull*
C. *Casino* | **D.** *Goodfellas*

$32,000

10. Who wrote the *Rabbit* novels, following the life of Rabbit Angstrom?

A. Philip Roth | **B.** John Irving
C. John Updike | **D.** Richard Adams

$64,000

11. In the movie *Harold and Maude,* what make of car does Harold customize into a hearse?

A. Porsche | **B.** Cadillac
C. Volkswagen | **D.** Jaguar

$125,000

12. Which is a weight class in boxing?

A. Straw
B. Grass
C. Leaf
D. Glass

$250,000

13. YYZ is the symbol for what city's airport?

A. Yokohama
B. Toronto
C. Yakima
D. Kabul

$500,000

14. Which economist wrote *The Road to Serfdom*?

A. Hans Sennholz
B. Milton Friedman
C. Ludwig von Mises
D. Friedrich Hayek

$1,000,000

15. In what would you most likely find a monocoque?

A. Bridge game
B. Swimming pool
C. Airplane
D. Orchestra

ANSWERS ◆ TO JOHN CARPENTER'S CHALLENGE #24

1. D. *Dictionary*
2. C. *Chlorine*
3. A. *2*
4. B. *Bacteria*
5. D. *FICA*
6. B. *Freud*
7. A. *The Crocodile Hunter*
8. B. *Red*
9. A. Guilty by Suspicion
10. C. *John Updike*
11. D. *Jaguar*
12. A. *Straw*
13. B. *Toronto*
14. D. *Friedrich Hayek*
15. C. *Airplane*

JOHN CARPENTER'S CHALLENGE 25

$100

1. Which item would you be most likely to buy at Victoria's Secret?

A. Toaster
B. Bra
C. Hammer
D. Computer

$200

2. According to the saying, a chain is only as strong as what?

A. Its maker
B. The temperature
C. Its weakest link
D. Its steel

$300

3. What was the animal named Lassie?

A. Shark
B. Dolphin
C. Dog
D. Seal

$500

4. Which of the following would you most likely see a chiropractor about?

A. Slipped disk
B. Blurred vision
C. Flu
D. Kleptomania

$1,000

5. What is a dinghy?

A. Crab trap
B. Seaweed
C. Barnacle
D. Boat

$2,000

6. Which state contains the Badlands?

A. Idaho
B. South Dakota
C. Montana
D. North Dakota

$4,000

7. A coral ring left by a sunken volcano is known as what?

A. Atoll
B. Trench
C. Archipelago
D. Reef

$8,000

8. Of the following, which is highest in Cub Scout rank?

A. Wolf
B. Bobcat
C. Eagle
D. Bear

$16,000

9. What constellation is featured on the Australian flag?

A. Southern Cross
B. Cancer
C. Orion
D. Scorpio

$32,000

10. Who was the first American president born west of the Appalachians?

A. Herbert Hoover
B. Abraham Lincoln
C. Ulysses S. Grant
D. John Tyler

$64,000

11. Something vespine resembles a what?

A. Termite
B. Hornet
C. Wasp
D. Locust

$125,000

12. What country's flag is a solid field of green?

A. Libya **B.** Bahrain
C. Saudi Arabia **D.** Zambia

$250,000

13. Which of the following bands did *not* contain Eric Clapton?

A. The New Yardbirds **B.** Cream
C. Derek and the Dominos **D.** Blind Faith

$500,000

14. Which is the only remaining original member of the Dow Jones Industrial Average?

A. General Electric **B.** 3M
C. U.S. Steel **D.** Procter & Gamble

$1,000,000

15. On what sitcom did Jerry Seinfeld make his acting debut?

A. *Soap* **B.** *Three's Company*
C. *Benson* **D.** *Happy Days*

ANSWERS ◆ TO JOHN CARPENTER'S CHALLENGE #25

1. B. *Bra*
2. C. *Its weakest link*
3. C. *Dog*
4. A. *Slipped disk*
5. D. *Boat*
6. B. *South Dakota*
7. A. *Atoll*
8. D. *Bear*
9. A. *Southern Cross*
10. B. *Abraham Lincoln*
11. C. *Wasp*
12. A. *Libya*
13. A. *The New Yardbirds*
14. A. *General Electric*
15. C. Benson

25 TESTS FOR JOHN CARPENTER AND READERS

What follow are 25 tests of progressively difficult questions created by author and college philosophy professor Dr. Rod L. Evans. Like the questions created by John, the following questions cover diverse areas and should appeal to people of various interests. John has taken the tests. Although he correctly answered most of the questions, he missed some of them, indicated by asterisks (*) alongside the correct answers. Your task is to answer correctly at least as many questions as John. At the end of each test you will learn not only the correct answers but also the questions he missed. Good luck on matching wits against the "Million-Dollar Mind."

CHALLENGE 1

$100

1. How many items are in a dozen?

A. 6
B. 10
C. 12
D. 20

$200

2. What should you avoid putting into a microwave oven?

A. Paper
B. Food
C. Pizza
D. Metal

$300

3. Which is an example of a citrus fruit?

A. Grapefruit
B. Apple
C. Banana
D. Raisin

$500

4. What is the last book of the Bible?

A. Matthew
B. Revelation
C. John
D. Deuteronomy

$1,000

5. Which one of the following continents is crossed by the equator?

A. North America
B. Asia
C. South America
D. Australia

$2,000

6. On the TV show *Star Trek,* what color is Mr. Spock's blood?

   A. Blue **B.** Red
   C. Yellow **D.** Green

$4,000

7. Which mythological figure fell in love with his own reflection?

   A. Narcissus **B.** Hermes
   C. Sisyphus **D.** Ares

$8,000

8. Where was Andy Griffith's Mayberry supposed to be?

   A. Virginia **B.** South Carolina
   C. North Carolina **D.** Georgia

$16,000

9. In what year did the Dow Jones average top 2000?

   A. 1983 **B.** 1984
   C. 1986 **D.** 1987

$32,000

10. Who was the first female comic ever to be invited to sit on Johnny Carson's couch during her first appearance on *The Tonight Show*?

    A. Ellen Degeneres **B.** Rosie O'Donnell
    C. Roseanne Barr **D.** Joan Rivers

$64,000

11. Which person was *not* born in South Dakota?

    A. George McGovern **B.** Crazy Horse
    C. Hubert Humphrey **D.** Buffalo Bill

$125,000

12. How tall is Agatha Christie's Belgian detective Hercule Poirot?

    A. 5'4" **B.** 5'5"
    C. 5'6" **D.** 5'7"

$250,000

13. When Michael Jordan retired on January 13, 1999, how many seasons had he been the NBA's leading scorer?

    A. 8 **B.** 9
    C. 10 **D.** 11

$500,000

14. According to *Guinness World Records 2000*, where is the largest casino in the world?

    A. Connecticut **B.** Nevada
    C. New Jersey **D.** Florida

$1,000,000

15. How many miles can light travel in one year?

    A. 5.8 billion **B.** 58 billion
    C. 580 billion **D.** 5.8 trillion

ANSWERS ◆ TO CHALLENGE #1

1. C. *12*
2. D. *Metal*
3. A. *Grapefruit*
4. B. *Revelation*
5. C. *South America*
***6.** D. *Green*
7. A. *Narcissus*
8. C. *North Carolina*
***9.** D. *1987*
10. A. *Ellen Degeneres*
11. D. *Buffalo Bill (Wyoming)*
***12.** A. *5'4"*
***13.** C. *10*
14. A. *Connecticut*
***15.** D. *5.8 trillion*

CHALLENGE 2

$100

1. Who is pictured on the American one-dollar bill?

A. Jefferson
B. Washington
C. Lincoln
D. Ross Perot

$200

2. Of the following, which is most likely to serve as a police dog?

A. Poodle
B. Dachshund
C. Chihuahua
D. German shepherd

$300

3. Which of the following was in the movie *Gone With the Wind*?

A. Errol Flynn
B. Gene Hackman
C. Clark Gable
D. Humphrey Bogart

$500

4. Which is a common name for a mixed drink?

A. Screwdriver
B. Wrench
C. Hammer
D. Plunger

$1,000

5. On what day of the week did Robinson Crusoe meet his future faithful servant?

A. Thursday
B. Friday
C. Saturday
D. Sunday

$2,000

6. What percent alcohol is 86-proof bourbon?

A. 86 **B.** 8.6
C. 43 **D.** 14

$4,000

7. Who taught Aristotle?

A. Plato **B.** Socrates
C. Heraclitus **D.** Pericles

$8,000

8. What are people from Iowa called?

A. Buckeyes **B.** Cornhuskers
C. Hawkeyes **D.** Cyclones

$16,000

9. Where is Vanderbilt University?

A. Missouri **B.** North Carolina
C. Georgia **D.** Tennessee

$32,000

10. In computing, how many bits make a byte?

A. 4 **B.** 6
C. 8 **D.** 10

$64,000

11. What is comedian and actor Albert Brooks's original name?

A. Albert Einstein **B.** Albert Bernstein
C. Albert Bornstein **D.** Albert Bronstein

$125,000

12. From a town in what country did cantaloupes get their name?

A. Spain | **B.** Italy
C. Portugal | **D.** France

$250,000

13. In the 1974 movie *Airport '75,* what movie was shown aboard Columbia Airlines Flight 409?

A. *The French Connection* | **B.** *The Godfather*
C. *American Graffiti* | **D.** *The Sting*

$500,000

14. How many electoral votes did William Taft receive in the 1912 American presidential election?

A. 8 | **B.** 18
C. 28 | **D.** 38

$1,000,000

15. What was the first name of rock star J. P. Richards (the Big Bopper)?

A. John | **B.** Jason
C. Jape | **D.** Jay

ANSWERS ◆ TO CHALLENGE #2

1. B. *Washington*
2. D. *German shepherd*
3. C. *Clark Gable*
4. A. *Screwdriver*
5. B. *Friday*
6. C. *43*
7. A. *Plato*
8. C. *Hawkeyes*
9. D. *Tennessee*
10. C. *8*
11. A. *Albert Einstein (No kidding!)*
*12. B. *Italy*
*13. C. *American Graffiti*
*14. A. *8*
*15. C. *Jape*

CHALLENGE 3

$100

1. To what political party does Albert Gore belong?

   A. Democrat
   B. Republican
   C. Communist
   D. Endless Recount

$200

2. Which is a breed of cat?

   A. German shepherd
   B. Siamese
   C. Poodle
   D. Catfish

$300

3. At what age do Jewish boys normally receive a Bar Mitzvah?

   A. 11
   B. 12
   C. 13
   D. 14

$500

4. With which scandal was Richard Nixon associated?

   A. Teapot Dome
   B. Abscam
   C. Whitewater
   D. Watergate

$1,000

5. Darjeeling is a tea especially associated with what country?

   A. India
   B. Peru
   C. China
   D. Pakistan

$2,000

6. In what century was the TV series *Star Trek* set?

A. Twenty-first | **B.** Twenty-second
C. Twenty-third | **D.** Twenty-fourth

$4,000

7. How old was Huckleberry Finn in Mark Twain's novel?

A. 12 | **B.** 13
C. 14 | **D.** 15

$8,000

8. In what year did Sally Ride become the first American woman in space?

A. 1979 | **B.** 1981
C. 1983 | **D.** 1984

$16,000

9. Where was Calvin Coolidge born?

A. New Hampshire | **B.** Vermont
C. Maine | **D.** Massachusetts

$32,000

10. In the James Bond movie *Goldfinger*, what was Oddjob's nationality?

A. Chinese | **B.** Korean
C. Japanese | **D.** Thai

$64,000

11. How many amendments are in the current U.S. Constitution?

A. 24 | **B.** 25
C. 26 | **D.** 27

$125,000

12. Where was the Sundance Kid (Harry Longbaugh) born?

A. Utah | **B.** New Mexico
C. New York | **D.** Pennsylvania

$250,000

13. In the comic strip *Batman*, what is the last name of Alfred the butler?

A. Pennyworth | **B.** Billingsley
C. Farnsworth | **D.** Jennings

$500,000

14. What is the only major American university named after a teenager?

A. Harvey Mudd | **B.** Ogelthorpe
C. Stanford | **D.** Brown

$1,000,000

15. How many electoral votes did Ronald Reagan receive in 1984?

A. 470 | **B.** 490
C. 515 | **D.** 525

ANSWERS ◆ TO CHALLENGE #3

1. A. *Democrat*
2. B. *Siamese*
3. C. *13*
4. D. *Watergate*
5. A. *India*
6. C. *Twenty-third*
*7. B. *13*
*8. C. *1983*
9. B. *Vermont*
10. B. *Korean*
*11. D. *27*
12. D. *Pennsylvania*
13. A. *Pennyworth*
*14. C. *Stanford (named after Leland Stanford, Jr., whose memory was honored by railroad tycoon Leland Stanford, Sr.)*
15. D. *525*

CHALLENGE 4

$100

1. What sort of food is veal parmigiana?

   A. Italian
   B. Chinese
   C. Mexican
   D. Jewish

$200

2. Which planet is closest to the sun?

   A. Pluto
   B. Neptune
   C. Mars
   D. Mercury

$300

3. What travels fastest?

   A. Jet plane
   B. Light
   C. Sound
   D. Bullet

$500

4. What ocean is the largest?

   A. Pacific
   B. Atlantic
   C. Indian
   D. Arctic

$1,000

5. On the TV show *The Honeymooners*, what was Ralph Kramden's job?

   A. Cab driver
   B. Sewer worker
   C. Construction worker
   D. Bus driver

$2,000

6. Where in the U.S. is the Pro Football Hall of Fame?

   A. New York **B.** California
   C. Ohio **D.** Florida

$4,000

7. Who wrote the play *Pygmalion*?

   A. Albee **B.** Ionesco
   C. Chekhov **D.** Shaw

$8,000

8. Where is Brown University?

   A. Rhode Island **B.** New Jersey
   C. Massachusetts **D.** Connecticut

$16,000

9. In what year did John Paul II become the first non-Italian pope elected to the papacy in 455 years?

   A. 1975 **B.** 1977
   C. 1978 **D.** 1979

$32,000

10. What is the second oldest Ivy League university?

    A. Princeton **B.** Yale
    C. University of Pennsylvania **D.** Columbia

$64,000

11. How many people signed the Declaration of Independence?

    A. 39 **B.** 43
    C. 56 **D.** 59

$125,000

12. Which saint is known as the Angelic Doctor?

A. St. Augustine **B.** St. Luke
C. St. Ambrose **D.** St. Thomas Aquinas

$250,000

13. In what year did Alfred E. Newman first appear on the cover of *Mad* magazine?

A. 1955 **B.** 1956
C. 1957 **D.** 1958

$500,000

14. According to Greek mythology, who was the youngest Titan?

A. Cronus **B.** Hyperion
C. Mnemosyne **D.** Tethys

$1,000,000

15. What was the size of the ruby slippers worn by Dorothy in the movie *The Wizard of Oz*?

A. 4½ **B.** 5
C. 5½ **D.** 6

ANSWERS ◆ TO CHALLENGE #4

1. A. *Italian*
2. D. *Mercury*
3. B. *Light*
4. A. *Pacific*
5. D. *Bus driver*
6. C. *Ohio*
7. D. *Shaw*
8. A. *Rhode Island*
9. C. *1978*
***10.** B. *Yale*
***11.** C. *56*
12. D. *St. Thomas Aquinas*
***13.** B. *1956*
14. A. *Cronus*
15. A. *4½*

CHALLENGE 5

$100

1. Which president served before all the others?

A. Truman **B.** Wilson
C. McKinley **D.** Jefferson

$200

2. What ocean borders California?

A. Atlantic **B.** Pacific
C. Indian **D.** Arctic

$300

3. What is the highest mountain?

A. Mt. Everest **B.** Mt. McKinley
C. Mt. Blanc **D.** Mt. Kosciusko

$500

4. From what country did the U.S. buy Alaska?

A. France **B.** Spain
C. England **D.** Russia

$1,000

5. Where is the largest reef, the Great Barrier Reef?

A. South America **B.** Australia
C. North America **D.** Africa

$2,000

6. Gascony is a historical region of what country?

   A. France | **B.** Germany
   C. Italy | **D.** Spain

$4,000

7. How many pieces of silver did Judas Iscariot receive?

   A. 20 | **B.** 25
   C. 30 | **D.** 50

$8,000

8. How many ounces were in the original 7 Up bottle?

   A. 6½ | **B.** 7
   C. 10 | **D.** 12

$16,000

9. What job did Michael Crichton have before he made it as an author?

   A. Lawyer | **B.** Medical school professor
   C. Anthropology professor | **D.** Editorial writer

32,000

10. What state had no signers of the United States Constitution?

   A. Rhode Island | **B.** New York
   C. Connecticut | **D.** New Jersey

$64,000

11. What is TV personality Larry King's original last name?

   A. Zeiger | **B.** Cohen
   C. Koenig | **D.** Zetlin

$125,000

12. What was the title of Yoko Ono's 1971 book?

A. *Rubyfruit*
B. *Grapefruit*
C. *Tangerine*
D. *Apple*

$250,000

13. By what age did George Armstrong Custer become a Brigadier General during the Civil War?

A. 23
B. 24
C. 25
D. 26

$500,000

14. What American president is pictured on the million-dollar treasury bond?

A. Grant
B. T. Roosevelt
C. Madison
D. McKinley

$1,000,000

15. What degree of U.S. gun salute is appropriate for arriving or departing generals of the military?

A. 13
B. 15
C. 17
D. 19

ANSWERS ◆ TO CHALLENGE #5

1. D. *Jefferson*
2. B. *Pacific*
3. A. *Mt. Everest*
4. D. *Russia*
5. B. *Australia*
6. A. *France*
7. C. *30*
8. B. *7*
***9.** C. *Anthropology professor*
10. A. *Rhode Island*
11. A. *Zeiger*
***12.** B. Grapefruit
***13.** A. *23*
***14.** B. *T. Roosevelt*
***15.** C. *17*

CHALLENGE 6

$100

1. What color is associated with the Irish?

   A. Blue
   B. Yellow
   C. Orange
   D. Green

$200

2. Which vessel is known for moving beneath the water's surface?

   A. Canoe
   B. Submarine
   C. Dinghy
   D. Rowboat

$300

3. Which is *not* the name of a chess piece?

   A. Knight
   B. Rook
   C. Bishop
   D. Cleric

$500

4. What actor portrayed a woman in *Tootsie*?

   A. Dustin Hoffman
   B. Jim Carrey
   C. John Belushi
   D. Dan Aykroyd

$1,000

5. The TV show *The Sopranos* was created for what network?

   A. Showtime
   B. Fox
   C. HBO
   D. TNT

$2,000

6. What is an escargot?

   A. Omelet
   B. Fish
   C. Beef
   D. Cooked snail

$4,000

7. Where is the capital of Pennsylvania?

   A. Pittsburgh
   B. Lancaster
   C. Harrisburg
   D. Philadelphia

$8,000

8. Who designed the Guggenheim museum?

   A. Frank Lloyd Wright
   B. Buckminster Fuller
   C. I. M. Pei
   D. Edward Stone

$16,000

9. When was the Great Fire of London?

   A. 1656
   B. 1662
   C. 1666
   D. 1686

$32,000

10. When was daylight saving time officially adopted in the U.S.A.?

   A. 1865
   B. 1918
   C. 1929
   D. 1933

$64,000

11. With what country was the macarena originally associated?

   A. Spain
   B. Mexico
   C. Colombia
   D. Brazil

$125,000

12. Which boxer was the original Great White Hope?

A. John L. Sullivan
B. Bob Fitzsimmons
C. Jim Jeffries
D. Gentleman Jim Corbett

$250,000

13. Which one of the following songs did Richard Nixon ask Johnny Cash to sing at the White House in 1972?

A. "Folsom Prison Blues"
B. "I Walk the Line"
C. "The Ballad of Ira Hayes"
D. "Welfare Cadillac"

$500,000

14. How long was the fastest pit stop by race car driver Bobby Unser?

A. 4 seconds
B. 5 seconds
C. 6 seconds
D. 7 seconds

$1,000,000

15. How many Academy Awards did *A Streetcar Named Desire* win?

A. 4
B. 5
C. 6
D. 7

ANSWERS ◆ TO CHALLENGE #6

1. D. *Green*
2. B. *Submarine*
3. D. *Cleric*
4. A. *Dustin Hoffman*
5. C. *HBO*
6. D. *Cooked snail*
7. C. *Harrisburg*
8. A. *Frank Lloyd Wright*
***9.** C. *1666*
***10.** B. *1918*
***11.** D. *Brazil*
***12.** C. *Jim Jeffries*
***13.** D. *"Welfare Cadillac"*
***14.** A. *4 seconds*
15. A. *4*

CHALLENGE 7

$100

1. Who created the comic strip *Peanuts*?

   A. Walt Kelly
   B. Charlie Brown
   C. Walter Lantz
   D. Charles Schulz

$200

2. What city is known as the Windy City?

   A. New York
   B. Pittsburgh
   C. Chicago
   D. Nashville

$300

3. What is the equivalent of 10 in Roman numerals?

   A. V
   B. X
   C. D
   D. C

$500

4. What celestial bodies are sometimes called minor planets?

   A. Comets
   B. Novas
   C. Yellow dwarfs
   D. Asteroids

$1,000

5. "A little learning is a dangerous thing" is from a poem by which person?

   A. Alexander Pope
   B. Ralph Waldo Emerson
   C. H. W. Longfellow
   D. Thomas Hardy

$2,000

6. What is the young of a deer called?

A. Foal

B. Pup

C. Joey

D. Fawn

$4,000

7. What is a group of whales called?

A. Army

B. Shoal

C. Pod

D. Herd

$8,000

8. In the game of pocket billiards or pool, what color is the four ball?

A. Purple

B. Orange

C. Blue

D. Red

$16,000

9. The Bolshevik revolt is associated with what month?

A. September

B. December

C. October

D. November

$32,000

10. How many incisors does an ordinary adult have?

A. 6

B. 8

C. 10

D. 12

$64,000

11. Where was the Teapot Dome, the Navy oil reserve involved in the scandal?

A. New Mexico

B. Arizona

C. Colorado

D. Wyoming

$125,000

12. What was Chico Marx's real first name?

A. Leonard | **B.** Adolph
C. Milton | **D.** Herbert

$250,000

13. Where did Lt. Col. Henry Blake attend college, according to the TV series *M*A*S*H*?

A. University of Indiana | **B.** Ball State University
C. University of Illinois | **D.** Purdue University

$500,000

14. What was the first country to ratify the U.N. Charter?

A. U.S. | **B.** France
C. New Zealand | **D.** Nicaragua

$1,000,000

15. In which Bugs Bunny cartoon did Bugs first use the line "Eh, what's up, Doc?"

A. "Elmer's Candid Camera" | **B.** "A Wild Hare"
C. "Elmer's Pet Rabbit" | **D.** "Tortoise Beats Hare"

ANSWERS ◆ TO CHALLENGE #7

1. D. *Charles Schulz*
2. C. *Chicago*
3. B. *X*
4. D. *Asteroids*
5. A. *Alexander Pope*
6. D. *Fawn*
7. C. *Pod*
*8. A. *Purple*
9. C. *October (It is often known as the October Revolution.)*
*10. B. *8*
11. D. *Wyoming*
12. A. *Leonard*
13. C. *University of Illinois*
*14. D. *Nicaragua*
15. B. *"A Wild Hare"*

CHALLENGE 8

$100

1. Where is the Empire State Building?

A. New York
B. New Jersey
C. Connecticut
D. Delaware

$200

2. What part of speech are the words *tree, car*, and *movie*?

A. Adjective
B. Noun
C. Preposition
D. Verb

$300

3. When was Pearl Harbor bombed?

A. 1898
B. 1914
C. 1933
D. 1941

$500

4. Of what state was Ronald Reagan the governor?

A. Texas
B. California
C. Arizona
D. Washington

$1,000

5. In what year did the Great Depression begin, marked by the stock market crash?

A. 1927
B. 1928
C. 1929
D. 1930

$2,000

6. What American state contains the most people?

A. Texas
B. New York
C. California
D. Florida

$4,000

7. When was the first Super Bowl game played?

A. 1966
B. 1967
C. 1968
D. 1969

$8,000

8. Where is Ft. Sumter?

A. Charleston, South Carolina
B. Pittsburgh, Pennsylvania
C. Cheyenne, Wyoming
D. Baltimore, Maryland

$16,000

9. How many stories (*not* sides) are in the Pentagon?

A. 4
B. 5
C. 6
D. 7

$32,000

10. In the American army, what is the maximum number of soldiers in a squad?

A. 6
B. 8
C. 10
D. 12

$64,000

11. What did Florence Nightingale keep in her pocket?

A. Sparrow
B. Robin
C. Hamster
D. Owl

$125,000

12. For what college team did football player Jim Brown set a scoring record in 1956?

A. Grambling
B. University of Southern California
C. Ohio State
D. Syracuse

$250,000

13. Normally, how many eggs will a hummingbird lay during its lifetime?

A. 2
B. 5
C. 10
D. 12

$500,000

14. Based on a computer analysis, what is the most frequently landed-on square in the game of Monopoly?

A. Go
B. B & O Railroad
C. Illinois Avenue
D. Free Parking

$1,000,000

15. How many times did jockey Bill Shoemaker win the Preakness Stakes?

A. 2
B. 3
C. 4
D. 5

ANSWERS ◆ TO CHALLENGE #8

1. A. *New York*
2. B. *Noun*
3. D. *1941*
4. B. *California*
5. C. *1929*
6. C. *California*
***7.** B. *1967 (though it wasn't called the Super Bowl until 1969)*
8. A. *Charleston, South Carolina*
***9.** B. *5*
***10.** C. *10*
***11.** D. *Owl*
12. D. *Syracuse*
***13.** A. *2*
***14.** C. *Illinois Avenue*
15. A. *2*

CHALLENGE 9

$100

1. What show did Johnny Carson host?

   A. *To Tell the Truth* **B.** *Jeopardy*
   C. *Hollywood Squares* **D.** *The Tonight Show*

$200

2. What is the name of Fred Flintstone's wife?

   A. Alice **B.** Trixie
   C. Wilma **D.** Betty

$300

3. In which state is the city of Seattle?

   A. Wisconsin **B.** Washington
   C. Maine **D.** Michigan

$500

4. Which car manufacturer produces the Mustang?

   A. Chevrolet **B.** Chrysler
   C. Ford **D.** Cadillac

$1,000

5. How many symphonies did Beethoven compose?

   A. 9 **B.** 8
   C. 7 **D.** 6

$2,000

6. How many sides does a quindecagon have?

A. 12 **B.** 15
C. 20 **D.** 24

$4,000

7. Which expedition first landed people on the moon?

A. Apollo 8 **B.** Apollo 10
C. Apollo 11 **D.** Apollo 13

$8,000

8. Who was the first American president to throw out the first ball of the baseball season?

A. T. Roosevelt **B.** Taft
C. Wilson **D.** Hoover

$16,000

9. In what current country is the former kingdom of Bohemia?

A. Austria **B.** Hungary
C. Germany **D.** Czechoslovakia

$32,000

10. In a modern symphony orchestra, how many cellos are there?

A. 6 **B.** 9
C. 12 **D.** 16

$64,000

11. What is the name of the kangaroo trademark used by Pocket Books?

A. Hoppy **B.** Selma
C. Shirley **D.** Gertrude

$125,000

12. How long did it take Lindbergh to fly across the Atlantic?

A. 33.5 hours **B.** 35 hours
C. 37 hours **D.** 37.5 hours

$250,000

13. According to the *U.S. Federal Motor Vehicle Safety Standard*, how far in feet will the average passenger car traveling on a non-slide surface be able to stop when going 80 mph?

A. 216 **B.** 405
C. 607 **D.** 673

$500,000

14. What is the highest number of touchdowns O. J. Simpson scored in one season?

A. 20 **B.** 21
C. 22 **D.** 23

$1,000,000

15. Who was the only individual in *Rowan & Martin's Laugh-In* to win an Emmy?

A. Arte Johnson **B.** Goldie Hawn
C. Judy Carne **D.** Henry Gibson

ANSWERS ◆ TO CHALLENGE #9

1. D. *The Tonight Show*
2. C. *Wilma*
3. B. *Washington*
4. C. *Ford*
5. A. *9*
*6. B. *15*
*7. C. *Apollo 11*
*8. B. *Taft*
9. D. *Czechoslovakia*
10. C. *12*
11. D. *Gertrude*
12. A. *33.5 hours*
13. B. *405*
14. D. *23*
*15. A. *Arte Johnson*

CHALLENGE 10

$100

1. According to the Bible, who was the first man?

   A. Cain
   B. Adam
   C. Aaron
   D. Moses

$200

2. What is the lowest denomination of bills in Monopoly?

   A. $1
   B. $5
   C. $10
   D. $20

$300

3. What is a contract called that is spoken but *not* written?

   A. Oral
   B. Aural
   C. Oval
   D. Actual

$500

4. What is the only crime defined in the U.S. Constitution?

   A. Bribery
   B. Obstruction of justice
   C. Assault
   D. Treason

$1,000

5. In the song "The Twelve Days of Christmas," how many maids are "a-milking"?

   A. 6
   B. 7
   C. 8
   D. 9

$2,000

6. Who wrote *The Divine Comedy*?

   A. Shakespeare **B.** Chaucer
   C. Milton **D.** Dante

$4,000

7. Throughout most of the Civil War, what was the capital of the Confederacy?

   A. Montgomery, Alabama **B.** Richmond, Virginia
   C. Danville, Virginia **D.** Atlanta, Georgia

$8,000

8. Who was the only Heisman trophy winner to play for a team with a losing record?

   A. Doak Walker **B.** George Rogers
   C. Paul Hornung **D.** Terry Baker

$16,000

9. From a town in what state did Fig Newton cookies get their name?

   A. Massachusetts **B.** Iowa
   C. Kansas **D.** North Carolina

$32,000

10. At what angle is the number 5 golf iron?

    A. 21 degrees **B.** 24 degrees
    C. 27 degrees **D.** 31 degrees

$64,000

11. What is the traditional gift for the fortieth wedding anniversary?

    A. Pearl **B.** Sapphire
    C. Ruby **D.** Jade

$125,000

12. What flower is associated with the month of October?

A. Hops **B.** Hawthorn
C. Violet **D.** Chrysanthemum

$250,000

13. According to the Beaufort Scale, what is the maximum wind speed in miles per hour for a strong breeze?

A. 12–19 **B.** 20–28
C. 39–49 **D.** 50–61

$500,000

14. How many bones are in our ten fingers?

A. 20 **B.** 24
C. 28 **D.** 32

$1,000,000

15. What TV star in the 1960s became, at that time, the highest earning entertainer in the history of show business?

A. Dean Martin **B.** Jackie Gleason
C. Johnny Carson **D.** Ed Sullivan

ANSWERS ◆ TO CHALLENGE #10

1. B. *Adam*
2. A. *$1*
3. A. *Oral*
4. D. *Treason*
5. C. *8*
6. D. *Dante*
7. B. *Richmond, Virginia*
8. C. *Paul Hornung*
9. A. *Massachusetts*
10. C. *27 degrees*
***11.** C. *Ruby*
***12.** A. *Hops*
13. C. *39–49*
14. C. *28*
***15.** A. *Dean Martin (who signed a three-year, $34-million contract with NBC, and had earnings for records, Las Vegas appearances, and other income generators.)*

CHALLENGE 11

$100

1. On a standard pair of dice, what is the highest number one can roll?

   A. 4 **B.** 6
   C. 82 **D.** 12

$200

2. In what religion was Jesus reared?

   A. Buddhism **B.** Hinduism
   C. Judaism **D.** Islam

$300

3. Which person is a famous tennis player?

   A. Mary Lou Retton **B.** Peggy Fleming
   C. Louie Anderson **D.** Billie Jean King

$500

4. In what year was Bill Clinton elected President of the United States for his first term?

   A. 1988 **B.** 1992
   C. 1994 **D.** 1996

$1,000

5. In what state was Elvis Presley born?

   A. Missouri **B.** Georgia
   C. Mississippi **D.** Alabama

$2,000

6. Which group was the first Seattle-based grunge band to gain major national publicity?

   A. Mudhoney **B.** Hole
   C. Pearl Jam **D.** Nirvana

$4,000

7. Where is the United States Naval Academy?

   A. New London, Connecticut **B.** Annapolis, Maryland
   C. Baltimore, Maryland **D.** Kings Point, New York

$8,000

8. Who is credited with discovering penicillin?

   A. James Watson **B.** Alexander Fleming
   C. F.H. Crick **D.** Jonas Salk

$16,000

9. Which colored M&M is produced in the greatest quantities?

   A. Brown **B.** Red
   C. Yellow **D.** Orange

$32,000

10. In what year did the space shuttle *Challenger* explode?

    A. 1984 **B.** 1985
    C. 1986 **D.** 1987

$64,000

11. What group sang the one-hit wonder *Incense and Peppermints*?

    A. The Strawberry Alarm Clock **B.** The Status Quo
    C. Steam **D.** The Five Stair Steps

$125,000

12. What is Rush Limbaugh's middle name?

A. David | **B.** Howard
C. Franklin | **D.** Hudson

$250,000

13. What was the first name of the man on whose property was the original Woodstock Festival?

A. Max | **B.** Rich
C. Bill | **D.** Bob

$500,000

14. On what professional hockey team was the first goalie to score a goal?

A. Boston Bruins | **B.** Detroit Red Wings
C. Chicago Blackhawks | **D.** New York Islanders

$1,000,000

15. In what year did the Little League World Series begin?

A. 1939 | **B.** 1941
C. 1945 | **D.** 1949

ANSWERS ♦ TO CHALLENGE #11

1. D. *12*
2. C. *Judaism*
3. D. *Billie Jean King*
4. B. *1992*
5. C. *Mississippi*
6. D. *Nirvana*
7. B. *Annapolis, Maryland*
8. B. *Alexander Fleming*
9. A. *Brown*
*10. C. *1986*
11. A. *The Strawberry Alarm Clock*
*12. D. Hudson
13. A. *Max* (*Yasgur*)
14. D. *New York Islanders* (Goalie Bill Smith scored *a goal in 1979.*)
15. A. *1939*

CHALLENGE 12

$100

1. Which of the following words names a variety of apple?

   A. Bartlett
   B. Delicious
   C. Pie
   D. Turnover

$200

2. Which American president was killed in office?

   A. Tyler
   B. Taft
   C. Lincoln
   D. T. Roosevelt

$300

3. What does the science of genetics deal with?

   A. Heredity
   B. Theology
   C. Old age
   D. Hydroponics

$500

4. How long does a U.S. president serve for each term?

   A. 4 years
   B. 6 years
   C. 7 years
   D. 8 years

$1,000

5. Where is the city of Mecca?

   A. Egypt
   B. Turkey
   C. Saudi Arabia
   D. Syria

$2,000

6. With what candy did the children in the movie *E.T.* coax the extraterrestrial out of the shed?

A. Sugar Babies
B. Jelly beans
C. M&Ms
D. Reese's Pieces

$4,000

7. Which is the largest of the Great Lakes?

A. Huron
B. Michigan
C. Superior
D. Ontario

$8,000

8. How many bones does an ordinary adult have?

A. 197
B. 206
C. 232
D. 236

$16,000

9. How many time zones are in China?

A. 1
B. 3
C. 4
D. 5

$32,000

10. In what year did Sonny Liston lose his title to Muhammad Ali (Cassius Clay)?

A. 1962
B. 1963
C. 1964
D. 1965

$64,000

11. In what year did Americans substitute the Gregorian calendar for the Julian one?

A. 1688
B. 1752
C. 1776
D. 1800

$125,000

12. How many times did Franklin Roosevelt carry his home county, Dutchess County, in his four presidential elections?

A. 4 | **B.** 3
C. 2 | **D.** 0

$250,000

13. What sort of handgun killed Robert Kennedy?

A. A .357 magnum | **B.** A .38 special
C. A 9 millimeter | **D.** A .22-caliber revolver

$500,000

14. Of the eight Ivy League colleges, which one has had the same name throughout its history?

A. Columbia | **B.** Cornell
C. Princeton | **D.** Harvard

$1,000,000

15. In what year was French adopted as the official language of Quebec?

A. 1975 | **B.** 1976
C. 1977 | **D.** 1978

ANSWERS ◆ TO CHALLENGE #12

1. B. *Delicious*
2. C. *Lincoln*
3. A. *Heredity*
4. A. *4 years*
5. C. *Saudi Arabia*
6. D. *Reese's Pieces*
7. C. *Superior*
8. B. *206*
9. A. *1*
*10. C. *1964*
*11. B. *1752*
12. D. *0*
*13. D. *A .22-caliber revolver*
14. B. *Cornell*
*15. C. *1977*

CHALLENGE 13

$100

1. Which weighs the most?

A. Cat
B. Dog
C. Peacock
D. Whale

$200

2. Whose picture is on the U.S. ten-dollar bill?

A. Lincoln's
B. Jackson's
C. Hamilton's
D. Grant's

$300

3. In which time zone of the U.S. is Virginia?

A. Eastern
B. Central
C. Mountain
D. Pacific

$500

4. Who said "Give me liberty or give me death"?

A. George Washington
B. Samuel Adams
C. Thomas Jefferson
D. Patrick Henry

$1,000

5. Which city is known as the City of Brotherly Love?

A. Cleveland
B. San Francisco
C. New York
D. Philadelphia

$2,000

6. Which man was a heavyweight boxer?

A. Rocky Graziana
B. Joe Louis
C. Henry Armstrong
D. Sugar Ray Robinson

$4,000

7. Which of the following is *not* one of the states representing the Four Corners of southwest America?

A. Colorado
B. Arizona
C. Kansas
D. New Mexico

$8,000

8. What are athletic teams from Princeton University called?

A. Crimson
B. Tigers
C. Cavaliers
D. Buckeyes

$16,000

9. How many Old Testament books are in the King James Version of the Bible?

A. 35
B. 37
C. 39
D. 41

$32,000

10. Which person was *not* born in North Carolina?

A. Booker T. Washington
B. Billy Graham
C. Dolley Madison
D. Edward R. Murrow

$64,000

11. Who was known as Mr. Republican?

A. Abraham Lincoln
B. Teddy Roosevelt
C. Robert A. Taft
D. Thomas Dewey

$125,000

12. What number represents the total number of daughters of presidents Kennedy, Johnson, Nixon, Ford, Carter, and Clinton?

A. 8 **B.** 9
C. 10 **D.** 11

$250,000

13. What state is sometimes known as the Freestone State?

A. New Hampshire **B.** Connecticut
C. Pennsylvania **D.** Arizona

$500,000

14. What was the estimated value of the twelve works of art stolen from the Isabella Stewart Gardner Museum in Boston in 1990?

A. $30 million **B.** $45 million
C. $75 million **D.** $100 million

$1,000,000

15. Which sport was originally called sphairistike?

A. Badminton **B.** Lawn tennis
C. Croquet **D.** Polo

ANSWERS ♦ TO CHALLENGE #13

1. D. *Whale*
2. C. *Hamilton's*
3. A. *Eastern*
4. D. *Patrick Henry*
5. D. *Philadelphia*
6. B. *Joe Louis*
7. C. *Kansas*
8. B. *Tigers*
9. C. *39*
***10.** A. *Booker T. Washington*
***11.** C. *Robert A. Taft*
***12.** A. *8*
13. B. *Connecticut*
***14.** D. *$100 million*
***15.** B. *Lawn tennis ("Sphairistike" is from sphaira, Greek for "lawn.")*

CHALLENGE 14

$100

1. What is the capital of France?

   A. Paris
   B. Toulouse
   C. Nice
   D. Cognac

$200

2. Whom did John F. Kennedy defeat to become president?

   A. Eisenhower
   B. Dewey
   C. Goldwater
   D. Nixon

$300

3. Who was a Greek philosopher?

   A. Descartes
   B. Hume
   C. Hegel
   D. Plato

$500

4. What state is known as the Green Mountain State?

   A. Virginia
   B. Vermont
   C. Washington
   D. Oregon

$1,000

5. In what city is the University of Virginia?

   A. Norfolk
   B. Richmond
   C. Charlottesville
   D. Lexington

$2,000

6. How many members are on a lacrosse team?

   A. 6 **B.** 7
   C. 9 **D.** 10

$4,000

7. What is the chemical symbol for silver?

   A. Si **B.** Sr
   C. S **D.** Ag

$8,000

8. What was the name of the high school represented on such TV shows as *Happy Days, Mr. Novak*, and *Mr. Peepers*?

   A. Whitman High **B.** Jefferson High
   C. Carver High **D.** Madison High

$16,000

9. In which state will you find a hundred-mile stretch of road called the Extraterrestrial Highway?

   A. Colorado **B.** New Mexico
   C. Arizona **D.** Nevada

$32,000

10. For what profession was Josef Stalin studying before he became a Marxist?

   A. Mechanical engineering **B.** Civil engineering
   C. Law **D.** Priesthood

$64,000

11. What state is sometimes known as the Flickertail State?

   A. Minnesota **B.** Washington
   C. North Dakota **D.** South Dakota

$125,000

12. How many gold medals did Jesse Owens win in the 1936 Olympics?

A. 2 **B.** 3
C. 4 **D.** 5

$250,000

13. What was the name of the steamship that brought the Statue of Liberty from France to New York in 1885?

A. *Irene* **B.** *Marie*
C. *Minette* **D.** *Evette*

$500,000

14. When was Hamburger Helper first marketed?

A. 1968 **B.** 1970
C. 1974 **D.** 1976

$1,000,000

15. What was the first country to make car seat belts compulsory?

A. Czechoslovakia **B.** Japan
C. Australia **D.** Ivory Coast

ANSWERS ♦ TO CHALLENGE #14

1. A. *Paris* ***6.** D. *10* **11.** C. *North Dakota*
2. D. *Nixon* **7.** D. *Ag* **12.** C. *4*
3. D. *Plato* ***8.** B. *Jefferson High* ***13.** A. Irene
4. B. *Vermont* **9.** D. *Nevada* ***14.** B. *1970*
5. C. *Charlottesville* **10.** D. *Priesthood* **15.** A. *Czechoslovakia*

$100

1. People on a low-sodium diet should be careful to watch their intake of what?

   A. Sugar
   B. Pepper
   C. Rat poison
   D. Salt

$200

2. Of what state was George W. Bush the governor?

   A. Texas
   B. Virginia
   C. New Mexico
   D. Arizona

$300

3. Which of the following has the fewest calories?

   A. Radishes
   B. Cucumber
   C. Water
   D. Apples

$500

4. In what book of the Bible is the Creation discussed?

   A. Leviticus
   B. Numbers
   C. Genesis
   D. Exodus

$1,000

5. How many teeth does an ordinary adult have?

   A. 29
   B. 30
   C. 31
   D. 32

$2,000

6. Who played Dracula in the 1931 movie of that name?

A. Boris Karloff
B. Bela Lugosi
C. Lon Chaney, Sr.
D. Lon Chaney, Jr.

$4,000

7. Who was the first American in space?

A. Alan Shepard
B. John Glenn
C. Virgil Grissom
D. Edwin Aldrin

$8,000

8. What constellation is called the Hunter?

A. Pisces
B. Scorpio
C. Pegasus
D. Orion

$16,000

9. What is the only state with an official state emblem?

A. Virginia
B. Texas
C. Utah
D. Maryland

$32,000

10. In what year did New Orleans Saint Tom Dempsey kick a 63-yard field goal?

A. 1968
B. 1969
C. 1970
D. 1971

$64,000

11. With whose band was Merv Griffin most closely associated?

A. Glenn Miller
B. Tommy Dorsey
C. Artie Shaw
D. Freddy Martin

$125,000

12. Where was the fictional character Philip Marlowe born?

A. California **B.** Washington
C. Oregon **D.** Arizona

$250,000

13. What was the name of the projected German invasion of Great Britain in the Second World War?

A. Operation Overlord **B.** Operation Sea Lion
C. Operation Lightning **D.** Operation Overflight

$500,000

14. Which animal sleeps the most, excluding periods of hibernation?

A. Opossum **B.** Sloth
C. Koala **D.** Armadillo

$1,000,000

15. In which season in the 1980s did Wayne Gretsky score the most goals?

A. 1981–1982 **B.** 1982–1983
C. 1983–1984 **D.** 1984–1985

ANSWERS ♦ TO CHALLENGE #15

1. D. *Salt*
2. A. *Texas*
3. C. *Water*
4. C. *Genesis*
5. D. *32*
6. B. *Bela Lugosi*
***7.** A. *Alan Shepard*
8. D. *Orion*
9. C. *Utah (the Beehive, signifying Mormon industriousness)*
***10.** C. *1970 (Nov. 8, against the Detroit Lions)*
***11.** D. *Freddy Martin*
12. A. *California*
13. B. *Operation Sea Lion*
14. C. *Koala (averaging 22 hours of sleep a day)*
15. A. *1981–1982 (when Gretsky scored 92 goals)*

CHALLENGE 16

$100

1. Which is the smallest U.S. state?

A. Vermont
B. New Jersey
C. Maryland
D. Rhode Island

$200

2. In what month is the American Thanksgiving?

A. September
B. October
C. November
D. December

$300

3. Of the following, which planet is farthest from the sun?

A. Venus
B. Earth
C. Jupiter
D. Neptune

$500

4. What element is contained in water?

A. Neon
B. Hydrogen
C. Sodium
D. Carbon

$1,000

5. What is the name of the wife of former senator Robert Dole?

A. Elizabeth
B. Laura
C. Nancy
D. Susan

$2,000

6. Who is the Greek equivalent of the Roman god Mercury?

   A. Hermes
   B. Ares
   C. Cronus
   D. Hephaestus

$4,000

7. In what religion was the Buddha reared?

   A. Buddhism
   B. Zoroastrianism
   C. Hinduism
   D. Judaism

$8,000

8. How many years was *All in the Family* the top-rated TV show?

   A. 3
   B. 4
   C. 5
   D. 6

$16,000

9. In 1976, which movie won the Academy Award for Best Picture?

   A. *Annie Hall*
   B. *One Flew Over the Cuckoo's Nest*
   C. *Network*
   D. *Rocky*

$32,000

10. What are the first names of the Everly Brothers?

    A. Don and Phil
    B. Bob and Dave
    C. Ben and Jim
    D. Rob and Dave

$64,000

11. In what year did French women gain the right to vote?

    A. 1908
    B. 1912
    C. 1922
    D. 1944

$125,000

12. What was the name of the fort from which George Armstrong Custer departed May 17, 1876, on his way to the Little Big Horn?

A. Fort Franklin Pierce **B.** Fort Andrew Jackson
C. Fort Zachary Taylor **D.** Fort Abraham Lincoln

$250,000

13. According to the comic books, who was the father of Porky Pig?

A. Phred **B.** Phineas
C. Phillip **D.** Pokey

$500,000

14. Who is known as the Singing Sheriff?

A. Bill Monroe **B.** Sonny James
C. Faron Young **D.** Roy Rogers

$1,000,000

15. What is the smallest number of states a candidate can win in a presidential election and receive at least 270 electoral votes?

A. 12 **B.** 13
C. 14 **D.** 15

ANSWERS ◆ TO CHALLENGE #16

1. D. *Rhode Island*
2. C. *November*
3. D. *Neptune*
4. B. *Hydrogen*
5. A. *Elizabeth*
6. A. *Hermes*
7. C. *Hinduism*
8. C. *5*
***9.** D. *Rocky*
10. A. *Don and Phil*
11. D. *1944*
12. D. *Fort Abraham Lincoln*
13. B. *Phineas*
14. C. *Faron Young*
15. A. *12*

CHALLENGE 17

$100

1. Where would a person be expected to wear a wig?

   A. Head
   B. Hand
   C. Feet
   D. His chimney

$200

2. With what team was Babe Ruth most famously associated?

   A. New York Yankees
   B. Pittsburgh Pirates
   C. Boston Red Sox
   D. Brooklyn Dodgers

$300

3. What is the capital of Massachusetts?

   A. Cambridge
   B. Boston
   C. Lexington
   D. Provincetown

$500

4. What does the *P* represent in the TV network PBS?

   A. Private
   B. Public
   C. Philadelphia
   D. Pittsburgh

$1,000

5. When did Jay Leno take over *The Tonight Show*?

   A. 1989
   B. 1991
   C. 1992
   D. 1993

$2,000

6. How many American presidents were assassinated in office?

A. 2 **B.** 3
C. 4 **D.** 5

$4,000

7. How high is the basket ring in basketball?

A. 10 feet **B.** 12 feet
C. 14 feet **D.** 15 feet

$8,000

8. What is the number on B.D.'s football jersey in the comic strip *Doonesbury*?

A. 5 **B.** 6
C. 8 **D.** 10

$16,000

9. In what year did the Brooklyn Dodgers move to L.A.?

A. 1955 **B.** 1956
C. 1957 **D.** 1958

$32,000

10. What does a Brannock device do?

A. Measures people's feet **B.** Cuts metal pipe
C. Shapes clay **D.** Measures angles in carpentry

$64,000

11. When did actor Dick Sargent take over the part of Darrin Stephens from Dick York on the TV show *Bewitched*?

A. 1967 **B.** 1968
C. 1969 **D.** 1970

$125,000

12. Where was the 1942 Rose Bowl Game played?

A. Pasadena, California
B. Salem, Oregon
C. Durham, North Carolina
D. Berkeley, California

$250,000

13. What is the first name of attorney Wilson in Mark Twain's novel *The Tragedy of Pudd'nhead Wilson*?

A. Michael
B. Robert
C. Richard
D. David

$500,000

14. Where did Bill Cosby earn his Ed. D.?

A. Amherst College
B. Temple University
C. Penn State
D. University of Pittsburgh

$1,000,000

15. How many time zones are in South America?

A. 1
B. 2
C. 3
D. 4

ANSWERS ◆ TO CHALLENGE #17

1. A. *Head*
2. A. *New York Yankees*
3. B. *Boston*
4. B. *Public*
***5.** C. *1992*
6. C. *4*
7. A. *10 feet*
8. D. *10*
***9.** C. *1957*
10. A. *Measures people's feet*
11. C. *1969*
***12.** C. *Durham, North Carolina (Oregon State defeated Duke 20 to 16.)*
***13.** D. *David*
14. A. *Amherst College*
15. C. *3*

CHALLENGE 18

$100

1. In which month is Halloween?

   A. July
   B. August
   C. September
   D. October

$200

2. With what war is the expression "the blue and the gray" associated?

   A. War of 1812
   B. American Civil War
   C. Spanish-American War
   D. World War II

$300

3. What automobile manufacturer produces the Camry?

   A. Honda
   B. Nissan
   C. Toyota
   D. Hyundai

$500

4. What does the Greek prefix *theo* mean?

   A. Human being
   B. Life
   C. Teacher
   D. God

$1,000

5. What U.S. president had a sign on his desk that read "The buck stops here"?

   A. Lincoln
   B. Kennedy
   C. Truman
   D. Eisenhower

$2,000

6. How long is a millennium?

   A. Ten years
   B. Hundred years
   C. One thousand years
   D. Ten thousand years

$4,000

7. What is the inflammation of the liver called?

   A. Colitis
   B. Cystitis
   C. Nephritis
   D. Hepatitis

$8,000

8. Which one of the following teams lost four consecutive Super Bowl games, 1991–1994?

   A. Buffalo Bills
   B. Washington Redskins
   C. New York Giants
   D. San Diego Chargers

$16,000

9. How was Genghis Khan related to Kublai Khan?

   A. Uncle to nephew
   B. Father to son
   C. Great-grandfather to great-grandson
   D. Grandfather to grandson

$32,000

10. What is the least old Ivy League university?

   A. Dartmouth
   B. Brown
   C. Cornell
   D. Columbia

$64,000

11. In what state was the setting of the film *To Kill a Mockingbird*?

   A. Georgia
   B. Alabama
   C. Mississippi
   D. Tennessee

$125,000

12. What was the jersey number of Paul Crewe, the character played by Burt Reynolds in the movie *The Longest Yard*?

A. 10 **B.** 12
C. 18 **D.** 22

$250,000

13. Which baseball team was known as having the $100,000 infield?

A. New York Yankees **B.** Philadelphia Athletics
C. Boston Red Sox **D.** Cincinnati Reds

$500,000

14. How long does it take Venus to rotate on its axis completely?

A. 58 days **B.** 88 days
C. 144 days **D.** 244 days

$1,000,000

15. When did Smokey the Bear die at the National Zoo in Washington, D.C.?

A. 1974 **B.** 1976
C. 1977 **D.** 1978

ANSWERS ◆ TO CHALLENGE #18

1. D. *October*
2. B. *American Civil War*
3. C. *Toyota*
4. D. *God*
5. C. *Truman*
6. C. *One thousand years*
7. D. *Hepatitis*
8. A. *Buffalo Bills*
9. D. *Grandfather to grandson*
10. C. *Cornell (1865)*
***11.** B. *Alabama*
***12.** D. *22*
***13.** B. *Philadelphia Athletics*
***14.** D. *244 days*
***15.** B. *1976*

CHALLENGE 19

$100

1. Which fruit is usually green on the outside?

   A. Lemon | **B.** Raisin
   C. Prune | **D.** Lime

$200

2. Which food would most likely be sold at a Chinese restaurant?

   A. Mongolian beef | **B.** Pizza
   C. Taco | **D.** Corned beef sandwich

$300

3. How many moons does Earth have?

   A. 0 | **B.** 1
   C. 2 | **D.** 3

$500

4. Who was the president immediately before Lyndon Johnson?

   A. JFK | **B.** Nixon
   C. Eisenhower | **D.** Truman

$1,000

5. Where did Archie Bunker live?

   A. Philadelphia | **B.** Detroit
   C. Los Angeles | **D.** Queens, New York

$2,000

6. What is the name of the pirate in Peter Pan?

   A. Captain Hook
   B. Bluebeard
   C. Blackbeard
   D. Captain Queeg

$4,000

7. With what war is V-J Day associated?

   A. First World War
   B. Second World War
   C. Korean
   D. Vietnam

$8,000

8. From which country did the U.S. buy Louisiana?

   A. Spain
   B. Portugal
   C. France
   D. The Netherlands

$16,000

9. How many astronauts were on each Mercury flight?

   A. 0
   B. 1
   C. 2
   D. 3

$32,000

10. How many Apollo moon landings were there?

    A. 3
    B. 4
    C. 5
    D. 6

$64,000

11. With which economist was the expression "invisible hand" originally associated?

    A. Adam Smith
    B. David Ricardo
    C. Milton Friedman
    D. Friedrich Hayek

$125,000

12. How many professional fights did Gene Tunney lose?

A. 1	**B.** 2
C. 3	**D.** 4

$250,000

13. Where did the first McDonald's hamburger restaurant open?

A. Indiana	**B.** Illinois
C. Ohio	**D.** Michigan

$500,000

14. How tall was actor Michael Dunn, who played Dr. Loveless on the TV show *The Wild Wild West*?

A. 3'10"	**B.** 4'2"
C. 4'4"	**D.** 4'6"

$1,000,000

15. On the TV show *Dragnet*, what did the radio expression "415" represent?

A. Disturbing the peace	**B.** Burglary
C. Theft	**D.** Robbery

ANSWERS ◆ TO CHALLENGE #19

1. D. *Lime*
2. A. *Mongolian beef*
3. B. *1*
4. A. *JFK*
5. D. *Queens, New York*
6. A. *Captain Hook*
7. B. *Second World War ("Victory in Japan")*
8. C. *France*
9. B. *1*
***10.** D. *6*
11. A. *Adam Smith*
***12.** A. *1 (to Harry Greb)*
13. B. *Illinois (Des Plaines)*
***14.** A. *3'10"*
15. A. *Disturbing the peace*

CHALLENGE 20

$100

1. Which is *not* a fish?

A. Sturgeon
B. Flounder
C. Trout
D. Hamburger

$200

2. Which is an example of a star?

A. The sun
B. Jupiter
C. Saturn
D. Mercury

$300

3. Which of the Three Stooges had extremely curly hair?

A. Moe
B. Larry
C. Curly
D. Shemp

$500

4. How many U.S. senators does each state have?

A. 1
B. 2
C. 3
D. 4

$1,000

5. Who is on the American two-dollar bill?

A. Grant
B. Jefferson
C. Franklin
D. Madison

$2,000

6. Which planet is named after the Roman goddess of love?

   A. Venus
   B. Saturn
   C. Mercury
   D. Uranus

$4,000

7. Who wrote *A Tale of Two Cities*?

   A. Thomas Hardy
   B. Lewis Carroll
   C. Anthony Trollope
   D. Charles Dickens

$8,000

8. Where is Georgetown University?

   A. Washington, D.C.
   B. Virginia
   C. Delaware
   D. Maryland

$16,000

9. Who wrote *The Sun Also Rises*?

   A. Faulkner
   B. Twain
   C. Hemingway
   D. Dickens

$32,000

10. Which of the following is the second largest continent (in area)?

    A. Asia
    B. North America
    C. South America
    D. Africa

$64,000

11. Who wrote the poem *Prometheus Unbound*?

    A. Milton
    B. Keats
    C. Shelley
    D. Blake

$125,000

12. During the Second World War, what were American tugboats named after?

    A. Fish **B.** Gods
    C. Dead war heroes **D.** Indian tribes

$250,000

13. What is the traditional symbol of St. Luke?

    A. Ox **B.** Eagle
    C. Angel **D.** Lion

$500,000

14. On the show *Gilligan's Island,* what was the skipper character's real name?

    A. Jonas Grumby **B.** Roy Hinkley
    C. Russell Johnson **D.** Josh Billings

$1,000,000

15. What is a special name for a group of ferrets?

    A. Clamor **B.** Chattering
    C. Business **D.** Confusion

ANSWERS ◆ TO CHALLENGE #20

1. D. *Hamburger*
2. A. *The sun*
3. B. *Larry*
4. B. *2*
5. B. *Jefferson*
6. A. *Venus*
7. D. *Charles Dickens*
8. A. *Washington, D.C.*
9. C. *Hemingway*
10. D. *Africa*
***11.** C. *Shelley*
12. D. *Indian tribes*
***13.** A. *Ox*
14. A. *Jonas Grumby*
15. C. *Business*

CHALLENGE 21

$100

1. What is the expression for the practice of joining others in a meal or an amusement when each person pays for herself?

   A. Trick or treat **B.** German treat
   C. French treat **D.** Dutch treat

$200

2. What was English prime minister Mr. Churchill's first name?

   A. William **B.** Kevin
   C. Winston **D.** Reginald

$300

3. Who was nicknamed Uncle Joe by the British?

   A. Hitler **B.** Stalin
   C. Churchill **D.** Franklin Roosevelt

$500

4. What is the first letter of the Greek alphabet?

   A. Alpha **B.** Beta
   C. Omega **D.** Delta

$1,000

5. What is the Show-Me State?

   A. Mississippi **B.** Montana
   C. Missouri **D.** Minnesota

$2,000

6. How many original Mighty Morphin Power Rangers were there?

   A. 3
   B. 4
   C. 5
   D. 6

$4,000

7. In Greek mythology, who was Ares?

   A. The god of war
   B. The god of love
   C. The god of thunder
   D. The god of the sea

$8,000

8. In what year did *The Wizard of Oz* appear?

   A. 1938
   B. 1939
   C. 1940
   D. 1941

$16,000

9. Which state became the forty-seventh state to join the U.S.A.?

   A. New Mexico
   B. Arizona
   C. Oklahoma
   D. Utah

$32,000

10. What actor, after having a lung removed in 1963, said "I licked the Big C" (cancer)?

    A. Edward G. Robinson
    B. Yul Brynner
    C. John Wayne
    D. Steve McQueen

$64,000

11. According to the Bible, what was Mordecai's blood relation to Esther?

    A. Uncle
    B. Nephew
    C. Cousin
    D. Brother-in-law

$125,000

12. How did *U-2* pilot Gary Powers die?

A. In a car crash | **B.** In a helicopter crash
C. In a plane crash | **D.** In an accident inside his home

$250,000

13. How tall was Elwood P. Dowd's invisible friend, the Pooka, in the novel (and movie) *Harvey*?

A. 6' | **B.** 6'1½"
C. 6'3½" | **D.** 6'4"

$500,000

14. How many of Rocky Marciano's 50 professional fights did he win by knockout?

A. 37 | **B.** 39
C. 41 | **D.** 43

$1,000,000

15. What author originally wrote about the Cisco Kid?

A. O. Henry | **B.** Louis L'Amour
C. James Fennimore Cooper | **D.** Bret Harte

ANSWERS ◆ TO CHALLENGE #21

1. D. *Dutch treat*
2. C. *Winston*
3. B. *Stalin*
4. A. *Alpha*
5. C. *Missouri*
*6. C. *5*
7. A. *The god of war*
*8. B. *1939*
9. A. *New Mexico*
*10. C. *John Wayne*
*11. C. *Cousin*
*12. B. *In a helicopter crash* (while working as a traffic spotter for TV station KNBC in Los Angeles)
*13. C. *6'3½"*
14. D. *43*
15. A. *O. Henry*

CHALLENGE 22

$100

1. Someone who is working in secret is said to be working how?

   A. Inside cover
   B. Without cover
   C. Overboard
   D. Undercover

$200

2. From what does coffee come?

   A. Leaf
   B. Bean
   C. Bag
   D. Stalk

$300

3. During the American Revolutionary War, what were British soldiers called?

   A. Red Coats
   B. Blue Coats
   C. Yellow Coats
   D. Green Coats

$500

4. With what group of people are leprechauns associated?

   A. French
   B. Irish
   C. English
   D. Spanish

$1,000

5. Of what country was Anastasio Somoza a president?

   A. El Salvador
   B. Panama
   C. Nicaragua
   D. Honduras

$2,000

6. When did Richard Nixon resign from office?

A. 1972 **B.** 1973
C. 1974 **D.** 1975

$4,000

7. Who starred in the TV series *McCloud*?

A. James Garner **B.** Clint Walker
C. Dennis Weaver **D.** Mike Connors

$8,000

8. With what instrument was John Coltrane especially associated?

A. Guitar **B.** Saxophone
C. Clarinet **D.** Trumpet

$16,000

9. In what year did Egypt's Anwar Sadat die?

A. 1981 **B.** 1982
C. 1983 **D.** 1984

$32,000

10. What was the name of Robert E. Lee's horse?

A. Dignity **B.** Traveler
C. Rienzi **D.** Little Sorrel

$64,000

11. What English poet wrote *Khubla Khan*?

A. William Blake **B.** Percy Shelley
C. John Keats **D.** Samuel Coleridge

$125,000

12. How many days did the 1982 football strike last?

A. 43 **B.** 55
C. 57 **D.** 63

$250,000

13. If your glass contains Cointreau and Cognac, what might you be drinking?

A. A Rolls Royce **B.** A Flying Dutchman
C. A Temptation **D.** An Applecar

$500,000

14. What number was the Notre Dame football player George "the Gipper" Gipp?

A. 61 **B.** 63
C. 66 **D.** 68

$1,000,000

15. What artist hosted parties in which he stocked his pool with sea urchins?

A. Salvador Dali **B.** Andy Warhol
C. Basquiat **D.** Pablo Picasso

ANSWERS ◆ TO CHALLENGE #22

1. D. *Undercover*
2. B. *Bean*
3. A. *Red Coats*
4. B. *Irish*
5. C. *Nicaragua*
***6.** C. *1974*
***7.** C. *Dennis Weaver*
8. B. *Saxophone*
***9.** A. *1981*
10. B. *Traveler*
***11.** D. *Samuel Coleridge*
12. C. *57*
13. A. *A Rolls Royce*
***14.** C. *66*
15. A. *Salvador Dali*

CHALLENGE 23

$100

1. What is a group of sheep called?

A. Posse
B. Flock
C. Nide
D. Team

$200

2. How many sides does the Pentagon have?

A. 4
B. 5
C. 6
D. 7

$300

3. How many railroads are in the game of Monopoly?

A. 2
B. 3
C. 4
D. 5

$500

4. How many people are on the current U.S. Supreme Court?

A. 6
B. 7
C. 8
D. 9

$1,000

5. What was Ronald Reagan's favorite candy when he was president?

A. Jelly beans
B. Dark chocolate
C. Butterfinger bars
D. Caramel

$2,000

6. Who was known to "float like a butterfly, sting like a bee"?

   A. Sugar Ray Leonard **B.** Joe Louis
   C. Muhammad Ali **D.** Roberto Duran

$4,000

7. In the rock song, in what city is the House of the Rising Sun?

   A. San Francisco **B.** New Orleans
   C. Los Angeles **D.** New York

$8,000

8. Who sang Audrey Hepburn's singing parts in *My Fair Lady*?

   A. Debbie Reynolds **B.** Julie Andrews
   C. Patti Page **D.** Marni Nixon

$16,000

9. What is the profession of Charlie Brown's father?

   A. Barber **B.** Merchant
   C. Physician **D.** Realtor

$32,000

10. For what sport has the Lang Cup been given?

    A. Archery **B.** Skeet shooting
    C. Skiing **D.** Pistol shooting

$64,000

11. In the movie *Hud*, what was Hud's last name?

    A. Brandon **B.** Bannon
    C. Brown **D.** Brant

$125,000

12. What was the name of Lt. Columbo's wife?

A. Barbara
B. Louise
C. Betty
D. Mildred

$250,000

13. What is Gerald R. Ford's middle name?

A. Robert
B. Rudolph
C. Reese
D. Richard

$500,000

14. When did Toucan Sam of Kellogg's Fruit Loops make his debut as their symbol?

A. 1961
B. 1962
C. 1963
D. 1964

$1,000,000

15. What college track team did future actor Bruce Dern quit because he refused to shave his sideburns?

A. Princeton's
B. Berkeley's
C. Yale's
D. University of Pennsylvania's

ANSWERS ◆ TO CHALLENGE #23

1. B. *Flock*
2. B. *5*
3. C. *4*
4. D. *9*
5. A. *Jelly beans*
6. C. *Muhammad Ali*
7. B. *New Orleans*
8. D. *Marni Nixon*
9. A. *Barber*
*10. C. *Skiing*
*11. B. *Bannon*
12. D. *Mildred*
*13. B. *Rudolph*
*14. C. *1963*
*15. D. *University of Pennsylvania's*

CHALLENGE 24

$100

1. In what game would you expect to see a knight and a queen?

   A. Chess
   B. Checkers
   C. Monopoly
   D. Scrabble

$200

2. What is the only continent that is also a country?

   A. Africa
   B. North America
   C. Asia
   D. Australia

$300

3. Where did Superman originate?

   A. Mars
   B. Krypton
   C. Venus
   D. Jupiter

$500

4. How many squares are on a chessboard?

   A. 44
   B. 64
   C. 84
   D. 94

$1,000

5. Who was the American president during the first moon walk?

   A. LBJ
   B. Nixon
   C. Ford
   D. Carter

$2,000

6. How many flavors make up Neapolitan ice cream?

A. 1
B. 2
C. 3
D. 4

$4,000

7. What car manufacturer created the Edsel?

A. General Motors
B. Ford
C. Chrysler
D. Studebaker

$8,000

8. In what city was John Lennon killed?

A. New York
B. Washington, D.C.
C. Los Angeles
D. San Francisco

$16,000

9. Who was known as the Man of a Thousand Faces?

A. Boris Karloff
B. Christopher Lee
C. Bela Lugosi
D. Lon Chaney, Sr.

$32,000

10. What was the first name of surveyor Dixon, of the Mason-Dixon team?

A. Charles
B. Robert
C. Jeremiah
D. Edward

$64,000

11. In what state is Smallville, where Superman grew up?

A. Illinois
B. Ohio
C. Nebraska
D. Kansas

$125,000

12. In the movie *Rebel Without a Cause*, what movie star was pictured in Plato's (Sal Mineo's) school locker?

A. Alan Ladd | **B.** Errol Flynn
C. Dick Powell | **D.** Cary Grant

$250,000

13. How many basic positions of the feet are there in ballet?

A. 3 | **B.** 4
C. 5 | **D.** 6

$500,000

14. What is the name of the *storyteller's* cat in Edgar Allen Poe's tale "The Black Cat"?

A. Diogenes | **B.** Pluto
C. Alexander | **D.** Socrates

$1,000,000

15. When was the fictional character Perry Mason born, according to Erle Stanley Gardner, his creator?

A. 1891 | **B.** 1901
C. 1911 | **D.** 1916

ANSWERS ◆ TO CHALLENGE #24

1. A. *Chess*
2. D. *Australia*
3. B. *Krypton*
4. B. *64*
5. B. *Nixon*
6. C. *3 (vanilla, chocolate, and strawberry)*
7. B. *Ford*
8. A. *New York*
***9.** D. *Lon Chaney, Sr.*
10. C. *Jeremiah*
11. A. *Illinois*
***12.** A. *Alan Ladd*
13. C. *5*
***14.** B. *Pluto*
15. A. *1891*

CHALLENGE 25

$100

1. Which beverage normally contains caffeine?

   A. Coffee
   B. Milk
   C. Orange juice
   D. Lemonade

$200

2. What is the name of Bill and Hillary Clinton's daughter?

   A. Chessie
   B. Cherise
   C. Chelsea
   D. Chrissy

$300

3. What is the only U.S. state surrounded by water?

   A. Texas
   B. Florida
   C. Rhode Island
   D. Hawaii

$500

4. Which president is pictured on the quarter?

   A. Lincoln
   B. Jackson
   C. Washington
   D. Kennedy

$1,000

5. What is the name of an expression that is literally self-contradictory?

   A. Oxymoron
   B. Simile
   C. Metaphor
   D. Hyperbole

$2,000

6. Who wrote *Death of a Salesman*?

A. Eugene O'Neill
B. Clifford Odets
C. Arthur Miller
D. Edward Albee

$4,000

7. Where is the Cotton Bowl played?

A. Dallas, Texas
B. El Paso, Texas
C. Houston, Texas
D. Corpus Christi, Texas

$8,000

8. In the TV show *Kojak*, what was Telly Savalas's favorite candy?

A. Milk Duds
B. Jelly beans
C. Mr. Goodbar
D. Tootsie Roll Pops

$16,000

9. Who founded the National Organization for Women (NOW)?

A. Betty Friedan
B. Germaine Greer
C. Gloria Steinem
D. Margaret Sanger

$32,000

10. In what year did *Leave It to Beaver* debut on TV?

A. 1955
B. 1956
C. 1957
D. 1959

$64,000

11. What was the first American state to secede from the Union?

A. South Carolina
B. Mississippi
C. Florida
D. Alabama

$132,000

12. How many magnums of champagne are in a Methuselah?

A. 4 **B.** 6
C. 8 **D.** 10

$250,000

13. According to Dante's *Divine Comedy*, what circle of Hell is reserved for gluttonous people?

A. Second **B.** Third
C. Fourth **D.** Fifth

$500,000

14. According to the Bible, under what kind of tree were Saul and his sons buried?

A. Upas **B.** Fig
C. Olive **D.** Oak

$1,000,000

15. According to the Chinese calendar, what animal will represent the year 2007?

A. Horse **B.** Monkey
C. Dog **D.** Boar

ANSWERS ◆ TO CHALLENGE #25

1. A. *Coffee*
2. C. *Chelsea*
3. D. *Hawaii*
4. C. *Washington*
5. A. *Oxymoron*
***6.** C. *Arthur Miller*
7. A. *Dallas, Texas*
8. D. *Tootsie Roll Pops*
9. A. *Betty Friedan*
***10.** C. *1957*
11. A. *South Carolina*
***12.** A. *4*
13. B. *Third*
14. D. *Oak*
15. D. *Boar*

THE WORLD'S TOUGHEST TRIVIA QUESTIONS:

50 TESTS FOR CRACKING YOUR WISDOM TEETH

What follow are 50 tests containing many of the toughest trivia questions you will see anywhere, a product of a collaboration between the authors. While readers will probably correctly answer some of the questions, it is very unlikely that most readers will answer even a third correctly. If you do average 5 out of 15 correct answers on most tests, you are remarkably knowledgeable. Should you average 7 or 8 out of 15 correct answers and are not the fictitious genius Will Hunting or *Parade* magazine's real genius, Marilyn vos Savant (possessor of the world's highest documented IQ), you're scary.

While doing well on these tests would demonstrate wide knowledge, correctly answering a lower percentage of questions would *not* demonstrate an unusual level of ignorance. We regard these tests not so much as a valid and reliable means for measuring knowledge as sources of entertainment, especially when given to a group of people in a relaxed social gathering.

$1,000,000 CHALLENGE 1

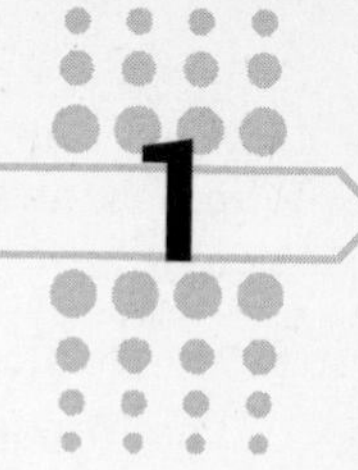

1. According to *World Almanac 2001*, which U.S. state, in 1990, had the third highest population density?

   A. New Jersey
   B. Massachusetts
   C. Connecticut
   D. Rhode Island

2. Which city in Virginia contains the most people?

   A. Norfolk
   B. Roanoke
   C. Richmond
   D. Virginia Beach

3. What was the last word given and spelled correctly in the Scripps Howard National Spelling Bee of 2000?

   A. Demarche
   B. Logorrhea
   C. Chiaroscurist
   D. Euonym

4. Which animal is fastest over approximate quarter-mile distances?

   A. Pronghorn antelope
   B. Wildebeest
   C. Quarter horse
   D. Zebra

5. According to *World Book 2001*, which of the following states contained more males than females in 1999?

   A. Utah
   B. New Mexico
   C. South Dakota
   D. California

6. Who was the second British rock group to have a number-one single in the U.S.?

   A. The Beatles
   B. The Animals
   C. The Tornadoes
   D. Manfred Mann

7. When did the United States Congress recognize American Indians as U.S. citizens?

   A. 1876
   B. 1880
   C. 1888
   D. 1924

8. Which popular single stayed number one on the pop chart the longest?

   A. "One Sweet Day" by Mariah Carey and Boys II Men
   B. "I Will Always Love You" by Whitney Houston
   C. "Candle in the Wind" by Elton John
   D. "Don't Be Cruel/Hound Dog" by Elvis Presley

9. When did Rush Limbaugh first register to vote?

   A. 1978
   B. 1980
   C. 1984
   D. 1988

10. Where did McDonald's open its first ski-through restaurant?

   A. Sweden
   B. Switzerland
   C. Colorado
   D. Norway

11. How much was John Scopes fined for having taught evolution?

   A. $50
   B. $75
   C. $100
   D. $150

12. What is a group of owls called?

A. Covert | **B.** Parliament
C. Covey | **D.** Tribe

13. Who was the first American president to be the object of an (unsuccessful) assassination attempt?

A. T. Roosevelt | **B.** Jackson
C. F. Roosevelt | **D.** Truman

14. Which school originated class rings?

A. Harvard | **B.** William and Mary
C. West Point | **D.** Yale

15. In the poem "Casey at the Bat," what was the final score?

A. 3 to 1 | **B.** 4 to 1
C. 4 to 0 | **D.** 4 to 2

ANSWERS ◆ TO $1,000,000 CHALLENGE #1

1. B. *Massachusetts*
2. D. *Virginia Beach*
3. A. *Demarche*
4. A. *Pronghorn antelope (about 61 mph)*
5. D. *California*
6. A. *The Beatles (Feb. 1, 1964; The Tornadoes were first with the instrumental "Tel-star," on Dec. 22, 1962.)*
7. D. *1924*
8. A. *"One Sweet Day" by Mariah Carey and Boys II Men*
9. D. *1988*
10. A. *Sweden (on the slopes of Lindvallen)*
11. C. *$100*
12. B. *Parliament*
13. B. *Jackson (in 1835, by Richard Lawrence, in the Capitol Rotunda)*
14. C. *West Point*
15. D. *4 to 2 (Casey's team, the Mudville Nine, lost to an anonymous team.)*

$1,000,000 CHALLENGE 2

1. How much was Pete Rose fined in 1990 for violating tax laws?

   A. $20,000 **B.** $30,000
   C. $40,000 **D.** $50,000

2. What was the name of Dorothy's pet cow in *The Wizard of Oz*?

   A. Imogene **B.** Margaret
   C. Bessie **D.** Alice

3. What is the northernmost state of the 48 contiguous states?

   A. Minnesota **B.** Maine
   C. Idaho **D.** Michigan

4. What is the first name of the model for the Statue of Liberty?

   A. Estelle **B.** Yvette
   C. Charlotte **D.** Dominique

5. Who failed to get the role of Captain Kirk on *Star Trek* because he insisted on owning part of the show?

   A. Robert Vaughn **B.** Jack Lord
   C. Burt Reynolds **D.** Mike Connors

6. What is Senator Edward M. Kennedy's middle name?

A. Michael **B.** Mitchell
C. Mark **D.** Moore

7. What was the original color of the cartoon bird Tweety Pie?

A. Yellow **B.** Blue
C. Pink **D.** Tan

8. How much is a pottle?

A. 2 pints **B.** 3 pints
C. 1 quart **D.** 2 quarts

9. What is the youngest age at which a female can legally marry in New Hampshire with her parents' consent?

A. 13 **B.** 14
C. 15 **D.** 16

10. What country consumes the most fat, according to the Food and Agricultural Organization of the UN?

A. Austria **B.** France
C. Belgium **D.** Italy

11. What were the most points scored by basketball player Michael Jordan in a single game?

A. 67 **B.** 69
C. 71 **D.** 73

12. Which king in a standard deck of playing cards has no mustache?

A. King of hearts | **B.** King of spades
C. King of clubs | **D.** King of diamonds

13. How old was the youngest person ever to have graduated from the Mt. Sinai School of Medicine in New York City?

A. 15 | **B.** 16
C. 17 | **D.** 19

14. Where were potato chips invented?

A. Saratoga Springs, New York | **B.** Paris, France
C. Boise, Idaho | **D.** Chicago, Illinois

15. In what year were toys added to boxes of Cracker Jacks?

A. 1893 | **B.** 1901
C. 1912 | **D.** 1921

ANSWERS ◆ TO $1,000,000 CHALLENGE #2

1. D. *$50,000*
2. A. *Imogene*
3. A. *Minnesota*
4. C. *Charlotte (mother of French sculptor Frederic Bartholdi)*
5. B. *Jack Lord*
6. D. *Moore*
7. C. *Pink (He was changed to yellow because censors complained that he looked naked as pink.)*
8. D. *2 quarts*
9. A. *13*
10. B. *France*
11. B. *69*
12. A. *King of hearts*
13. C. *17 (Balamurali Ambati of Hollis Hills, New York, became a doctor on May 19, 1995.)*
14. A. *Saratoga Springs, New York*
15. C. *1912*

$1,000,000 CHALLENGE 3

1. In what year did MTV make its debut?

   A. 1980 **B.** 1981
   C. 1982 **D.** 1983

2. What month is National Catfish Month and National Water Quality Month?

   A. June **B.** July
   C. August **D.** September

3. Who was the first American president to have a phone on his desk?

   A. Wilson **B.** Coolidge
   C. Hoover **D.** F.D.R.

4. How many rock bands appeared at the Woodstock Music and Art Fair?

   A. 12 **B.** 18
   C. 21 **D.** 24

5. What do L. L. Bean's initials stand for?

   A. Lesley Lawrence **B.** Laurence Lesley
   C. Louis Lindsey **D.** Leon Leonwood

6. In what city was the first modern traffic light?

   A. Chicago **B.** Cleveland
   C. Oklahoma City **D.** New York

7. Which city is the largest in area in the western hemisphere?

   A. Juneau, Alaska **B.** Jacksonville, Florida
   C. Los Angeles, California **D.** Houston, Texas

8. Where was the first U.S. medical school established?

   A. New York **B.** Chicago
   C. Philadelphia **D.** Boston

9. On a clear day how many states are visible from atop the Empire State Building?

   A. 3 **B.** 4
   C. 5 **D.** 6

10. How many inches is the diameter of a standard basketball hoop?

    A. 18 **B.** 20
    C. 22 **D.** 24

11. Where is the International Tennis Hall of Fame?

    A. Wimbledon (England) **B.** Rhode Island
    C. New York **D.** North Carolina

12. What is the principal element in Olympic gold medals?

A. Silver **B.** Gold
C. Nickel **D.** Copper

13. Which U.S. state has the most counties?

A. Georgia **B.** Kentucky
C. California **D.** Texas

14. In how many World Series games did Yogi Berra appear?

A. 45 **B.** 55
C. 65 **D.** 75

15. How many dimples are on a golf ball?

A. 286 **B.** 336
C. 386 **D.** 396

ANSWERS ♦ TO $1,000,000 CHALLENGE #3

1. B. *1981*
2. C. *August*
3. C. *Hoover*
4. D. *24*
5. D. *Leon Leonwood*
6. B. *Cleveland (in 1914)*
7. A. *Juneau, Alaska*
8. C. *Philadelphia (in 1765)*
9. C. *5 (New York, New Jersey, Connecticut, Massachusetts, and Pennsylvania)*
10. A. *18*
11. B. *Rhode Island (Newport)*
12. A. *Silver*
13. D. *Texas*
14. D. *75*
15. B. *336*

$1,000,000 CHALLENGE 4

1. Who appeared on the cover of *TV Guide* three weeks in a row?

   A. Michael Landon
   B. Jerry Seinfeld
   C. Carol Burnette
   D. Lucille Ball

2. Who appeared as the last act at Woodstock in 1969?

   A. Country Joe and the Fish
   B. Richie Havens
   C. Santana
   D. Jimi Hendrix

3. Which American president named his dog Veto to warn Congress against passing legislation he did not like?

   A. Hayes
   B. Fillmore
   C. Cleveland
   D. Garfield

4. What day of the week during the Second World War was recommended as a meatless day in the United States?

   A. Sunday
   B. Tuesday
   C. Wednesday
   D. Friday

5. What was Chuck Berry's first number-one hit?

   A. "My Ding-a-Ling"
   B. "Sweet Little Sixteen"
   C. "Roll Over Beethoven"
   D. "Johnny B. Goode"

6. What was the first name of Hoss Cartwright on the TV show *Bonanza*?

   A. Eric **B.** Samuel
   C. Robert **D.** James

7. Who is the only American president to have been sworn in by his father?

   A. Andrew Johnson **B.** Chester Arthur
   C. John Tyler **D.** Calvin Coolidge

8. What state was the last one to be readmitted into the Union after the Civil War?

   A. Mississippi **B.** Virginia
   C. Texas **D.** South Carolina

9. In what state was K-Mart founded?

   A. Michigan **B.** Arkansas
   C. Illinois **D.** Ohio

10. How many bones are in your big toe?

   A. 2 **B.** 3
   C. 4 **D.** 5

11. What was Alice Kramden's maiden name on the TV show *The Honeymooners*?

   A. Jenkins **B.** Russell
   C. Becker **D.** Gibson

12. What was Wrong Way Corrigan's real first name?

A. David
B. Douglas
C. Richard
D. Robert

13. What does *gung-ho* literally mean?

A. With enthusiasm
B. With fire
C. With strength
D. Work together

14. What was the first professional football team to introduce emblems on helmets?

A. Baltimore Colts
B. Chicago Bears
C. New York Giants
D. Los Angeles Rams

15. How many people did Billy the Kid kill, according to the inscription on his tombstone?

A. 12
B. 15
C. 21
D. 24

ANSWERS ◆ TO $1,000,000 CHALLENGE #4

1. A. *Michael Landon*
2. D. *Jimi Hendrix*
3. D. *Garfield*
4. B. *Tuesday*
5. A. *"My Ding-a-Ling" (That is his only number-one hit.)*
6. A. *Eric*
7. D. *Calvin Coolidge*
8. C. *Texas*
9. A. *Michigan (Detroit, in 1897)*
10. A. *2*
11. D. *Gibson*
12. B. *Douglas*
13. D. *Work together (from the Chinese)*
14. D. *Los Angeles Rams*
15. C. *21*

$1,000,000 CHALLENGE 5

1. What are Untorn Ribbon, Barber Perfect, and Underwood Tack?

   A. Pairs of scissors **B.** Barbed wire
   C. Tape **D.** Rope

2. What celebrity was originally named Bernard Schwartz?

   A. Tony Randall **B.** Eddie Cantor
   C. Milton Berle **D.** Tony Curtis

3. When did "The Star-Spangled Banner" become the official anthem of the United States?

   A. 1918 **B.** 1929
   C. 1931 **D.** 1933

4. About how long would the coils of a French horn be if they were straightened out?

   A. 12 feet **B.** 15 feet
   C. 18 feet **D.** 22 feet

5. How many operas did Wagner compose?

   A. 9 **B.** 11
   C. 13 **D.** 15

6. How many Chicago White Sox players were expelled from baseball because of the Black Sox scandal in 1919?

A. 5 **B.** 6
C. 7 **D.** 8

7. Who was originally supposed to play the role Humphrey Bogart played in *Casablanca*?

A. George Raft **B.** Joseph Cotton
C. George Brent **D.** Ronald Reagan

8. How many games did pitcher Cy Young win?

A. 491 **B.** 501
C. 511 **D.** 521

9. What was the last symphony Mozart composed?

A. *Jupiter* **B.** *Paris*
C. *Linz* **D.** *Haffner*

10. How much money did Bruce Springsteen turn down in 1986 from Lee Iococca, who wanted to use "Born in the U.S.A." for Chrysler commercials?

A. $4 million **B.** $8 million
C. $11 million **D.** $12 million

11. Who claimed in a 1993 *Rolling Stone* interview that, because of his practicing meditation, he can continuously make love for more than five hours?

A. John Travolta **B.** Sting
C. Tom Cruise **D.** Andrew Dice Clay

12. How many eggs did Lucas Jackson (Paul Newman) eat in *Cool Hand Luke*?

    A. 35 **B.** 38
    C. 42 **D.** 50

13. In what year did Frank Sinatra bring Dean Martin on stage at one of Jerry Lewis's telethons in Las Vegas?

    A. 1972 **B.** 1973
    C. 1975 **D.** 1976

14. What was the name of President Gerald Ford's golden retriever?

    A. Freedom **B.** Liberty
    C. Water boy **D.** Beachcomber

15. What is the license number of Donald Duck's car?

    A. 313 **B.** 515
    C. 616 **D.** 717

ANSWERS ◆ TO $1,000,000 CHALLENGE #5

1. B. *Barbed wire*
2. D. *Tony Curtis*
3. C. *1931*
4. D. *22 feet*
5. C. *13*
6. D. *8*
7. D. *Ronald Reagan*
8. C. *511*
9. A. *Jupiter*
10. D. *$12 million*
11. B. *Sting*
12. D. *50*
13. D. *1976*
14. B. *Liberty*
15. A. *313*

$1,000,000 CHALLENGE 6

1. Which one of the following athletes was *not* selected for two consecutive years as the male Athlete of the Year by sports editors from the Associated Press member newspapers?

   A. Joe DiMaggio **B.** Joe Montana
   C. Don Budge **D.** Carl Lewis

2. What is a gambado?

   A. A dance **B.** A fish
   C. A leap made by a horse **D.** A coat

3. How many years did singer Merle Haggard serve in San Quentin?

   A. 2 **B.** 3
   C. 4 **D.** 5

4. What was the first college football team to use uniform numbers?

   A. Notre Dame **B.** University of Minnesota
   C. Ohio State **D.** University of Pittsburgh

5. Of the American states in the Eastern time zone, how many are also in the Central time zone?

   A. 2 **B.** 3
   C. 4 **D.** 5

6. Who was the first black pitcher to win a World Series game?

   A. Don Black **B.** Satchel Paige
   C. Bob Gibson **D.** Joe Black

7. How many miles is a parsec?

   A. 5.8 trillion **B.** 11.6 trillion
   C. 16.4 trillion **D.** 19.2 trillion

8. In measurement of drinking alcohol, how much is a pony?

   A. .75 ounce **B.** 3 ounces
   C. 3.5 ounces **D.** 4.5 ounces

9. Which word means "sunbathing"?

   A. Decollation **B.** Scaphism
   C. Abacination **D.** Aprication

10. Who was cast as the lead in *Apocalypse Now* but was replaced by Martin Sheen after having a falling-out with director Francis Ford Coppola?

    A. Harvey Keitel **B.** Tommy Lee Jones
    C. Gene Hackman **D.** Brian Dennehy

11. Before becoming an actor, what government job did Dennis Franz have?

    A. Inspected buildings **B.** Delivered mail
    C. Worked as a bailiff **D.** Worked at a DMV

12. During the Second World War, what were cruisers usually named after?

    A. Dead war heroes　　**B.** Cities
    C. Gods of mythology　　**D.** Battles

13. Roughly how long did Brendan Fraser lift weights to beef up for his role in *George of the Jungle*?

    A. 2 months　　**B.** 3 months
    C. 6 months　　**D.** 9 months

14. What sort of athletic scholarship did Richard Gere win for college?

    A. Gymnastics　　**B.** Baseball
    C. Football　　**D.** Wrestling

15. In what Jerry Lewis movie did Colonel Sanders make a cameo appearance?

    A. *Artists and Models*　　**B.** *The Sad Sack*
    C. *The Disorderly Orderly*　　**D.** *The Loud Mouth*

ANSWERS ◆ TO $1,000,000 CHALLENGE #6

1. A. *Joe DiMaggio*
2. C. *A leap made by a horse*
3. B. 3
4. D. *University of Pittsburgh (December 5, 1908)*
5. C. *4 (Indiana, Kentucky, Tennessee, Florida)*
6. D. *Joe Black (won the first game of the 1952 World Series for the Brooklyn Dodgers)*
7. D. *19.2 trillion*
8. A. *.75 ounce*
9. D. *Aprication*
10. A. *Harvey Keitel*
11. B. *Delivered mail*
12. B. *Cities*
13. C. *6 months*
14. A. *Gymnastics*
15. D. The Loud Mouth

$1,000,000 CHALLENGE 7

1. Who was *not* one of the first three members of the Country Music Hall of Fame?

   A. Hank Williams　　**B.** Fred Rose
   C. Chet Atkins　　**D.** Jimmie Rodgers

2. Which was the first thoroughbred racehorse to win a million dollars?

   A. Native Dancer　　**B.** Secretariat
   C. Kelso　　**D.** Citation

3. What is the first name of comedian Flip Wilson?

   A. Carlton　　**B.** Cleavon
   C. Clerow　　**D.** Calvin

4. What does *cupidity* mean?

   A. Concupiscence　　**B.** Nisus
   C. Desideratum　　**D.** Gulosity

5. In what year was cigarette advertising banned from American TV?

   A. 1970　　**B.** 1971
   C. 1972　　**D.** 1973

6. What was the first single on the new label for The Rolling Stones on Rolling Stones Records?

A. "Tumbling Dice"
B. "Happy"
C. "You Can't Always Get What You Want"
D. "Brown Sugar"

7. Who was the only boxer who competed as a heavyweight but was outweighed by all his opponents?

A. Ingemar Johansson
B. Floyd Patterson
C. Max Schmelling
D. Jack Sharkey

8. The question "What's the frequency?" was in a song by R.E.M., who got the expression by hearing that it was used by two persons attacking what TV personality?

A. Morton Downey, Jr.
B. Queen Latifah
C. Dan Rather
D. Jerry Springer

9. When did Bob Dylan make his first New York appearance in eight years?

A. 1974
B. 1975
C. 1976
D. 1977

10. From what country did Angola gain its independence in 1975?

A. England
B. France
C. Spain
D. Portugal

11. In what year did the Rose Bowl end in a scoreless tie?

A. 1922
B. 1924
C. 1926
D. 1928

12. Which state is named after a valley in Pennsylvania?

A. Arkansas **B.** Wisconsin
C. Idaho **D.** Wyoming

13. Within how many days were there two assassination attempts on President Gerald Ford's life?

A. 17 **B.** 19
C. 21 **D.** 23

14. What is detective Nero Wolfe's favorite color?

A. Red **B.** Yellow
C. Green **D.** Purple

15. Who emceed the first Patsy Awards, given to animal actors?

A. Doris Day **B.** Betty White
C. Bob Barker **D.** Ronald Reagan

ANSWERS ◆ TO $1,000,000 CHALLENGE #7

1. C. *Chet Atkins*
2. D. *Citation*
3. C. *Clerow*
4. D. *Gulosity (greed)*
5. B. *1971*
6. D. *"Brown Sugar"*
7. B. *Floyd Patterson*
8. C. *Dan Rather*
9. A. *1974*
10. D. *Portugal*
11. A. *1922*
12. D. *Wyoming*
13. A. *17*
14. B. *Yellow*
15. D. *Ronald Reagan*

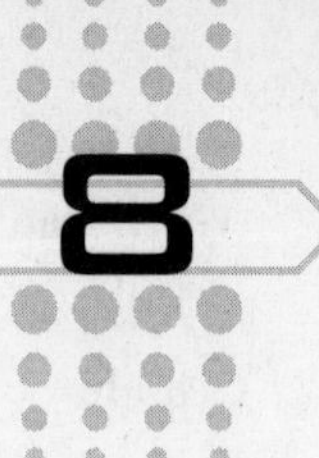

$1,000,000 CHALLENGE 8

1. Which baseball position did Snoopy play on Charlie Brown's team?

   A. Left field **B.** Shortstop
   C. Right field **D.** Center field

2. How many times was Kelsey Grammer nominated for an Emmy before finally receiving one in 1994?

   A. 2 **B.** 3
   C. 4 **D.** 5

3. In the old TV show *The Virginian,* in what state was the Shiloh ranch?

   A. Wyoming **B.** Arizona
   C. New Mexico **D.** Virginia

4. What item is designated number 44, especially in west coast restaurants in the 1940s?

   A. Hamburger **B.** Hot dog
   C. Coca-Cola **D.** Coffee

5. To what royal family did English King Richard III belong?

   A. Tudor **B.** Stuart
   C. Plantagenet **D.** York

6. Author John Grisham is said to be the sixteenth cousin of what politician?

   A. Bill Clinton
   B. Sam Nunn
   C. Dale Bumpers
   D. Trent Lott

7. In Scottish Rite Freemasonry, what degree is equivalent to a Grand Master Architect?

   A. 10th
   B. 11th
   C. 12th
   D. 13th

8. Which Shakespearean play was published after his death?

   A. *Henry V*
   B. *Troilus and Cressida*
   C. *Julius Caesar*
   D. *Sir John Falstaff and the Merry Wives of Windsor*

9. In what year did Raggedy Ann dolls first go on sale in the U.S.?

   A. 1913
   B. 1918
   C. 1922
   D. 1923

10. Which was introduced and marketed first?

   A. Barbie Doll
   B. Frisbee
   C. Scrabble
   D. Silly Putty

11. In what U.S. city was the first home refrigerator manufactured?

   A. Chicago
   B. New York
   C. Detroit
   D. Philadelphia

12. What would be the sum total of the number of President Gerald Ford's children, the number of American vice presidents who have resigned, and the number of Best Supporting Actor Academy Awards won by Walter Brennan?

A. 6	**B.** 7
C. 8	**D.** 9

13. What was the original name of Truth or Consequences, New Mexico?

A. Hot Springs	**B.** Gallup
C. Grants	**D.** Hobbs

14. What was the lifetime batting average of Ty Cobb?

A. .337	**B.** .347
C. .357	**D.** .367

15. When did chain letters promising instant wealth first appear in the U.S.?

A. 1918	**B.** 1929
C. 1933	**D.** 1935

ANSWERS ◆ TO $1,000,000 CHALLENGE #8

1. B. *Shortstop*
2. D. *5*
3. A. *Wyoming*
4. D. *Coffee*
5. D. *York*
6. A. *Bill Clinton*
7. C. *12th*
8. C. *Julius Caesar*
9. B. *1918*
10. C. *Scrabble (It was introduced in 1943, but it didn't become a fad until about 1961.)*
11. A. *Chicago (in 1913)*
12. D. *9 (4 + 2 + 3)*
13. A. *Hot Springs*
14. D. *.367*
15. D. *1935*

$1,000,000 CHALLENGE 9

1. Which is *not* a variety of pear?

   A. Flemish Beauty
   B. Alexander
   C. Muscadine
   D. Garlic

2. Which word represents a subfield of theology dealing specifically with the nature of faith?

   A. Pistology
   B. Eschatology
   C. Soteriology
   D. Theodicy

3. What is the middle name of John Anderson, who ran unsuccessfully as an independent presidential candidate in 1980?

   A. Douglas
   B. Bayard
   C. Joseph
   D. Alvin

4. Which ancient thinker believed that air is the most pervasive thing in the world?

   A. Anaximenes
   B. Anaximander
   C. Anaxagoras
   D. Thales

5. In what year was Idi Amin, former president of Uganda, overthrown?

   A. 1977
   B. 1978
   C. 1979
   D. 1980

6. What was the name of Elvis Presley's father?

A. William
B. John
C. George
D. Vernon

7. What disease did President Chester A. Arthur come to learn that he had after he took office?

A. Lung disease
B. Heart disease
C. Liver disease
D. Kidney disease

8. How many original S&H green trading stamps were needed to fill a book?

A. 800
B. 1000
C. 1200
D. 1500

9. What was the novel in which Sherlock Holmes first appeared?

A. *A Study in Scarlet*
B. *The Sign of Four*
C. *Scandal in Bohemia*
D. *Hound of the Baskervilles*

10. Who did *not* die in 1987?

A. Desi Arnaz
B. Liberace
C. Fred Astaire
D. Jackie Gleason

11. Where did the McCoys (of the feuding Hatfields and McCoys) live?

A. Virginia
B. West Virginia
C. Tennessee
D. Kentucky

12. In what year is the 1971 movie *The Omega Man* set?

A. 1977 **B.** 1985
C. 1989 **D.** 1997

13. What does *struthious* mean?

A. Pertaining to pigeons **B.** Pertaining to nightingales
C. Pertaining to ostriches **D.** Pertaining to grouses

14. How many years was Janet Reno chief prosecutor for Dade County, Florida?

A. 12 **B.** 13
C. 14 **D.** 15

15. What was the name of Robert Vaughn's character in *The Magnificent Seven*?

A. Britt **B.** Vin
C. Harry **D.** Lee

ANSWERS ◆ **TO $1,000,000 CHALLENGE #9**

1. B. *Alexander (peach)*
2. A. *Pistology*
3. B. *Bayard*
4. A. *Anaximenes*
5. C. *1979*
6. D. *Vernon*
7. D. *Kidney disease*
8. C. *1200*
9. A. A Study in Scarlet
10. A. *Desi Arnaz (1986)*
11. D. *Kentucky*
12. A. *1977*
13. C. *Pertaining to ostriches*
14. D. *15*
15. D. *Lee*

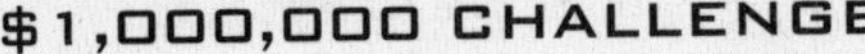

$1,000,000 CHALLENGE 10

1. Which U.S. president announced that he intended to run for a second term by throwing his hat into the center ring of a circus?

   A. Cleveland
   B. T. Roosevelt
   C. Wilson
   D. Taft

2. How much money did Nazi Herman Goering put on Clark Gable's head during the Second World War?

   A. $2,000
   B. $5,000
   C. $10,000
   D. $15,000

3. Who was not a *founding* member of the 1969 First Artists Production Company?

   A. Steve McQueen
   B. Paul Newman
   C. Barbra Streisand
   D. Sidney Poitier

4. What was Lieutenant Columbo's first name?

   A. Michael
   B. Jerry
   C. David
   D. Philip

5. In 1980, how did the character of Edith Bunker, of *All in the Family*, die?

   A. Heart attack
   B. Cancer
   C. Car accident
   D. Stroke

6. How long is a bowling alley?

A. 40 feet
B. 45 feet
C. 50 feet
D. 60 feet

7. What is the name of the doctor on whose book the TV show *M*A*S*H* was based?

A. Dr. Richard Hornberger
B. Dr. Robert Glaser
C. Dr. Bernard Einhorn
D. Dr. David Mayer

8. What was Mr. Smith's first name in the movie *Mr. Smith Goes to Washington*?

A. Eugene
B. Jefferson
C. Richard
D. Robert

9. In 1976, where was the convention in which 182 persons were infected by Legionnaires Disease?

A. New York
B. Los Angeles
C. Philadelphia
D. San Francisco

10. For what crime was Jack Nicholson's character imprisoned in the movie *One Flew Over the Cuckoo's Nest*?

A. Rape
B. Robbery
C. Burglary
D. Assault and battery

11. Off what state's coast did the movie *Jaws* take place?

A. California
B. New York
C. Massachusetts
D. Florida

12. What was the first brand of beer to be sold nationally in the U.S.?

A. Pabst Blue Ribbon
B. Miller
C. Schlitz
D. Budweiser

13. How many stars were on the American flag in 1818?

A. 17
B. 18
C. 19
D. 20

14. What sort of monster was the Japanese creature named Ebirah?

A. Gigantic shrimp
B. Gigantic jellyfish
C. Huge reptile
D. Huge turtle

15. How did author Ian Fleming arrive at the name James Bond?

A. From an author of a book
B. From a person he knew in the spy business
C. From a friend he knew from school
D. From a person he met in the military

ANSWERS ◆ TO $1,000,000 CHALLENGE #10

1. C. *Wilson*
2. B. *$5,000*
3. A. *Steve McQueen*
4. D. *Philip*
5. D. *Stroke*
6. D. *60 feet*
7. A. *Dr. Richard Hornberger*
8. B. *Jefferson*
9. C. *Philadelphia*
10. A. *Rape*
11. B. *New York (Long Island)*
12. D. *Budweiser*
13. D. *20*
14. A. *Gigantic shrimp*
15. A. *From an author of a book (on birds)*

$1,000,000 CHALLENGE 11

1. Who played first base for the Gashouse Gang in the 1930s?

   A. Pepper Martin
   B. Ducky Medwick
   C. Rip Collins
   D. Bill Delancy

2. In the TV series *Run for Your Life,* how long did Paul Bryan (Ben Gazzara) have to live?

   A. 6 months
   B. 1 year
   C. 2 years
   D. 3 years

3. What name does Benjamin Braddock (Dustin Hoffman) use to sign the Taft Hotel register on his first meeting with Mrs. Robinson (Anne Bancroft) in the movie *The Graduate*?

   A. Mr. Gladstone
   B. Mr. Churchill
   C. Mr. Wellington
   D. Mr. Chamberlain

4. What was Cool Hand Luke's prison number in the movie of that name?

   A. 32
   B. 35
   C. 37
   D. 39

5. How much money did the United States pay Denmark for the Danish Virgin Islands?

   A. $15,000,000
   B. $20,000,000
   C. $25,000,000
   D. $30,000,000

6. Who said "Strip the phony tinsel off Hollywood and you'll find the real tinsel underneath"?

   A. Bob Hope **B.** Oscar Levant
   C. Walter Winchell **D.** Groucho Marx

7. What was the "real" first name of the character called Penguin in *Batman*?

   A. Jack **B.** Mortimer
   C. Claude **D.** Oswald

8. What was the name of the character played by Mickey Rooney in the movie *It's a Mad, Mad, Mad, Mad World*?

   A. Lennie Pike **B.** Melville Crump
   C. Ding Bell **D.** Otto Meyer

9. Which philosopher is supposed to have said on his deathbed "Only one man understood me, and he didn't understand me"?

   A. Hegel **B.** Schopenhauer
   C. Kierkegaard **D.** Nietzsche

10. How many vertebrae are in a giraffe's neck?

    A. 7 **B.** 9
    C. 11 **D.** 13

11. What was the first automobile manufactured by the General Motors Corporation?

    A. Oldsmobile **B.** Chevrolet
    C. Buick **D.** Cadillac

12. As of 1973, about how many books were on the shelves of the Library of Congress in Washington, D.C.?

    A. 47,000,000 **B.** 57,000,000
    C. 62,000,000 **D.** 72,000,000

13. How many American mainland states have a coastline on either an ocean or gulf?

    A. 20 **B.** 22
    C. 23 **D.** 25

14. According to the U.S. Department of Agriculture, about how much U.S. land is owned by the federal government?

    A. One-fifth **B.** One-fourth
    C. One-third **D.** One-half

15. Who was the first member of the Monkees to quit the band?

    A. Davy Jones **B.** Mickey Dolenz
    C. Peter Tork **D.** Mike Nesmith

ANSWERS ◆ TO $1,000,000 CHALLENGE #11

1. C. *Rip Collins*
2. C. *2 years*
3. A. *Mr. Gladstone*
4. C. *37*
5. C. *$25,000,000*
6. B. *Oscar Levant*
7. D. *Oswald*
8. C. *Ding Bell*
9. A. *Hegel*
10. A. *7*
11. C. *Buick*
12. D. *72,000,000*
13. D. *25*
14. C. *One-third*
15. C. *Peter Tork*

$1,000,000 CHALLENGE 12

1. How many threads are in a bier?

   A. 30 **B.** 40
   C. 60 **D.** 100

2. What was Laura Petrie's maiden name on *The Dick Van Dyke Show*?

   A. Meehan **B.** Michaels
   C. Melvin **D.** Martin

3. How many stories below street level is CONTROL headquarters in the comedy TV show *Get Smart*?

   A. 10 **B.** 12
   C. 15 **D.** 20

4. Where did Rob Petrie originally meet Laura on *The Dick Van Dyke Show*?

   A. Ft. Sumter, South Carolina **B.** Ft. Bragg, North Carolina
   C. San Diego, California **D.** Joplin, Missouri

5. Where is Major Benjamin Franklin "Hawkeye" Pierce from, according to the TV show *M*A*S*H*?

   A. Indiana **B.** Maine
   C. Illinois **D.** Ohio

6. What crime did the character played by Elvis Presley allegedly commit in *Jailhouse Rock*?

A. Theft **B.** Robbery
C. Vandalism **D.** Murder

7. How much money did Alan Alda initially earn per episode on the TV show *M*A*S*H*?

A. $10,000 **B.** $15,000
C. $20,000 **D.** $25,000

8. What is Dr. Scholl's first name?

A. William **B.** Richard
C. Wallace **D.** Robert

9. When did the rock group Duran Duran begin their first American tour?

A. 1982 **B.** 1983
C. 1984 **D.** 1985

10. How many second violins are in a modern symphony orchestra?

A. 6 **B.** 9
C. 12 **D.** 16

11. In the movie *Twelve Angry Men*, which actor portrayed the head of a message service?

A. Martin Balsam **B.** John Fielder
C. Lee J. Cobb **D.** Robert Webber

12. In Goethe's *Faust*, for how many years of pleasure and knowledge did Dr. Faust sell his soul to the devil?

A. 24 **B.** 25
C. 50 **D.** 75

13. Which word means "living in holes"?

A. Fimicolous **B.** Arenicolous
C. Limicolous **D.** Latebricole

14. What time is on the clock in Independence Hall on the reverse side of the bicentennial 1776–1976 half-dollar?

A. 1:00 **B.** 3:00
C. 5:00 **D.** 9:00

15. Where is Darrin and Samantha Stephens's house, according to the TV show *Bewitched*?

A. Westport, Connecticut **B.** Pikesville, Maryland
C. Scarsdale, New York **D.** Columbus, Ohio

ANSWERS ◆ TO $1,000,000 CHALLENGE #12

1. B. *40*
2. A. *Meehan*
3. A. *10*
4. D. *Joplin, Missouri (at Camp Crowder, where she was a USO dancer)*
5. B. *Maine (Crabapple Cove)*
6. D. *Murder*
7. A. *$10,000*
8. A. *William*
9. C. *1984*
10. D. *16*
11. C. *Lee J. Cobb*
12. A. *24*
13. D. *Latebricole*
14. B. *3:00*
15. A. *Westport, Connecticut*

$1,000,000 CHALLENGE 13

1. Who invented a radio-controlled system to steer torpedoes?

   A. Marlene Dietrich **B.** Hedy Lamarr
   C. Celeste Holm **D.** Claudette Colbert

2. After an intersection in what city did astronaut Scott Carpenter name his *Aurora 7* capsule?

   A. Los Angeles, California **B.** Madison, Wisconsin
   C. Springfield, Illinois **D.** Boulder, Colorado

3. Where did Jimi Hendrix die?

   A. Paris **B.** Los Angeles
   C. Detroit **D.** London

4. What was Woodrow Wilson's middle name?

   A. Woodrow **B.** Thomas
   C. James **D.** Edward

5. In what year did Batman team up with Robin, the Boy Wonder?

   A. 1938 **B.** 1940
   C. 1942 **D.** 1944

6. Which river of Hades is called the river of lamentation?

   A. Acheron **B.** Styx
   C. Cocytus **D.** Lethe

7. How old was Lady Diana when her engagement to Prince Charles was announced?

   A. 19 **B.** 20
   C. 21 **D.** 22

8. In what year did the Miss America Pageant make its network TV debut?

   A. 1952 **B.** 1953
   C. 1954 **D.** 1955

9. How many teeth are in a male horse?

   A. 32 **B.** 34
   C. 36 **D.** 40

10. Who was the first president under whom F. B. I. director J. Edgar Hoover served?

    A. Wilson **B.** Harding
    C. Coolidge **D.** F. D. R.

11. Which American president rejected an honorary degree from Oxford because he didn't have a classical education and believed it inappropriate for anyone to "accept a degree he cannot read"?

    A. Taylor **B.** Fillmore
    C. Johnson **D.** Truman

12. How many consecutive shutout innings did Don Drysdale pitch for the Los Angeles Dodgers from May 14 to June 8, 1968?

    A. 54 **B.** 56
    C. 58 **D.** 59

13. What was gangster Dutch Schultz's real first name?

    A. Charles **B.** Arthur
    C. Richard **D.** Thomas

14. How much did General Tom Thumb, who was 36 inches tall, weigh at birth?

    A. 4 lbs. 4 oz. **B.** 5 lbs. 3 oz.
    C. 6 lbs. 2 oz. **D.** 9 lbs. 2 oz.

15. What was the flavor of the original filling in Hostess Twinkies?

    A. Vanilla **B.** Strawberry
    C. Chocolate **D.** Banana

ANSWERS ◆ TO $1,000,000 CHALLENGE #13

1. B. *Hedy Lamarr*
2. D. *Boulder, Colorado*
3. D. *London*
4. A. *Woodrow (Thomas was his first name.)*
5. B. *1940*
6. C. *Cocytus*
7. A. *19*
8. C. *1954*
9. D. *40*
10. B. *Harding (Hoover was originally assistant director.)*
11. B. *Fillmore*
12. C. *58*
13. B. *Arthur (Flegenheimer)*
14. D. *9 lbs. 2 oz.*
15. D. *Banana (The flavor was changed from banana to vanilla because of a banana shortage during World War II.)*

$1,000,000 CHALLENGE 14

1. Who was married the longest?

   A. Ernest Borgnine and Ethel Merman
   B. Patty Duke and Michael Tell
   C. Buck Owens and Jana Grief
   D. Rudolph Valentino and Jean Acker

2. How many states did Goldwater win in the 1964 presidential campaign against Johnson?

   A. 3
   B. 4
   C. 5
   D. 6

3. What was the first number-one Beatles hit in the U.S.?

   A. "I Want to Hold Your Hand"
   B. "She Loves You"
   C. "Please Please Me"
   D. "Twist and Shout"

4. Who was Sandy Koufax's father-in-law?

   A. Richard Widmark
   B. Ernie Kovacs
   C. Eddie Cantor
   D. Alfred T. Ringling

5. How many of Thomas Jefferson's children with his wife, Martha, died before he became president?

   A. 1
   B. 2
   C. 3
   D. 4

6. Who does not or did not have a minister for a father?

   A. Della Reese
   B. Dana Andrews
   C. John Hurt
   D. Alice Cooper

7. What do agyrophobes fear?

   A. Crossing the street
   B. Spinning
   C. Reversing themselves
   D. Losing their ability to turn

8. Who is the tallest?

   A. Brooke Shields
   B. Julia Child
   C. Geena Davis
   D. Carly Simon

9. In 1986, which one of the following people was *not* honored by the John F. Kennedy Center for the Performing Arts?

   A. Lucille Ball
   B. Ray Charles
   C. Bette Davis
   D. Yehudi Menuhin

10. How many points must a chess player earn to qualify as a grandmaster?

    A. 2200
    B. 2300
    C. 2500
    D. 2600

11. With which argument for the existence of God is St. Anselm associated?

    A. Ontological
    B. Teleological
    C. Cosmological
    D. Moral

12. What is the oldest U.S. college west of the Allegheny mountains?

A. Tulane University
B. Washington and Jefferson College
C. University of Cincinnati
D. The University of Iowa

13. Where did President Wilson attend law school?

A. University of Virginia
B. Harvard
C. Yale
D. Columbia

14. With what is gin combined to create a drink called a Red Lion?

A. Apricot Brandy
B. Sherry
C. Strawberries
D. Grand Marnier

15. Which movie did Victor Fleming *not* direct?

A. *The Wizard of Oz*
B. *Gone With the Wind*
C. *Great Expectations*
D. *Treasure Island*

ANSWERS ◆ TO $1,000,000 CHALLENGE #14

1. A. *Ernest Borgnine and Ethel Merman (3 weeks)*
2. D. 6
3. A. *"I Want to Hold Your Hand"*
4. A. *Richard Widmark*
5. D. *4 (of 6)*
6. A. *Della Reese (factory worker)*
7. A. *Crossing the street*
8. B. *Julia Child (6'2")*
9. C. *Bette Davis (1987)*
10. D. *2600*
11. A. *Ontological*
12. B. *Washington and Jefferson College (founded in 1781 in Washington, Pennsylvania)*
13. A. *University of Virginia*
14. D. *Grand Marnier*
15. C. Great Expectations

$1,000,000 CHALLENGE 15

1. Who was originally supposed to play Dirty Harry (Callahan) but was unable to play the character because of a wrist injury?

   A. Tom Selleck　　**B.** Frank Sinatra
   C. Jack Palance　　**D.** Richard Widmark

2. According to the Bible, what color of horse does Famine ride during the Apocalypse?

   A. Green　　**B.** Black
   C. White　　**D.** Red

3. According to tradition, what is the badge or symbol of the Christian apostle Thomas?

   A. A battleaxe　　**B.** A sword
   C. A saw　　**D.** A lance or spear

4. When did the Immaculate Conception (holding the Virgin Mother to have been conceived without Original Sin) become declared as an article of faith by the Roman Catholic Church?

   A. 1517　　**B.** 1592
   C. 1854　　**D.** 1870

5. Who is the only American president to die during a term in which both he *and* his wife died?

A. William Henry Harrison
B. James Garfield
C. William McKinley
D. Warren G. Harding

6. On the Réaumur scale, what temperature represents the boiling point of water?

A. 80°
B. 100°
C. 150°
D. 212°

7. In what year did *Reader's Digest* begin to carry advertisements?

A. 1922
B. 1930
C. 1933
D. 1955

8. How many Civil War battles did author Stephen Crane witness?

A. 0
B. 1
C. 2
D. 3

9. How many funerals did President James Garfield have?

A. 1
B. 2
C. 3
D. 4

10. What was author Theodore "Dr. Seuss" Geisel's middle name?

A. Seuss
B. Robert
C. Nicholas
D. Alexander

11. How many states were part of the United States in 1900?

A. 42 **B.** 43
C. 44 **D.** 45

12. As of the year 2000, who was the only American president to have been born on July 4?

A. Tyler **B.** Arthur
C. Fillmore **D.** Coolidge

13. How many years in prison was Al Capone sentenced for tax evasion?

A. 11 **B.** 15
C. 17 **D.** 24

14. What sort of brandy is Slivovitz?

A. Banana **B.** Plum
C. Apricot **D.** Peach

15. Where did Granny Smith apples originate?

A. England **B.** Washington
C. New South Wales (Australia) **D.** California

ANSWERS ◆ TO $1,000,000 CHALLENGE #15

1. B. *Frank Sinatra*
2. B. *Black* (Rev 6:5)
3. D. *A lance or spear (because he was said to have been pierced by a lance or spear)*
4. C. *1854 (by Pius IX)*
5. D. *Warren G. Harding*
6. A. *80°*
7. D. *1955*
8. A. *0*
9. C. *3 (one in Elberon, New Jersey, another in Washington, D.C., and the third in Cleveland, Ohio)*
10. A. *Seuss*
11. D. *45*
12. D. *Coolidge*
13. A. *11*
14. B. *Plum*
15. C. *New South Wales (Australia)*

$1,000,000 CHALLENGE 16

1. How many U.S. senators voted in favor of Justice Clarence Thomas's appointment to the U.S. Supreme Court?

   A. 51 **B.** 52
   C. 53 **D.** 54

2. What style of music did Mungo Jerry revive in 1970?

   A. Swamp rock **B.** Reggae
   C. Rockabilly **D.** Skiffle

3. Which Earp brother was wounded at the O.K. Corral?

   A. Virgil **B.** Morgan
   C. James **D.** Wyatt

4. Who was Clint Eastwood's character in *A Fistful of Dollars*?

   A. Joe **B.** Blondie
   C. Jed Cooper **D.** Rowdy

5. From what state did the puppet Howdy Doody hail?

   A. Wyoming **B.** Oklahoma
   C. Texas **D.** Arizona

6. Which word means "pitcher-shaped"?

   A. Panduriform | **B.** Clithiform
   C. Urceolate | **D.** Remiform

7. From 1960 to 1993, how many Rose Bowl championships involved teams that were scoreless?

   A. 0 | **B.** 1
   C. 2 | **D.** 3

8. What was the name of the character called Professor on *Gilligan's Island*?

   A. Roy Hinkley | **B.** Jonas Grumby
   C. Ridgely Hardy | **D.** Bob Richards

9. What does *jentacular* mean?

   A. Pertaining to the knee | **B.** Pertaining to refreshment
   C. Pertaining to irregular movement | **D.** Pertaining to breakfast

10. In how many movies did Elvis Presley appear?

   A. 28 | **B.** 29
   C. 30 | **D.** 31

11. On the TV show *The Fugitive,* what was Dr. Richard Kimble's medical specialty?

   A. Pediatrics | **B.** General medicine
   C. Neurosurgery | **D.** Obstetrics

12. Whose 1988 autobiography is entitled *Too Much Is Not Enough*?

    A. Orson Bean
    B. Shelley Winters
    C. Jackie Gleason
    D. Joan Collins

13. How many times was Richard Burton nominated for an Oscar?

    A. 5
    B. 6
    C. 7
    D. 8

14. At what institution was Phi Beta Kappa, the national honorary academic society, founded?

    A. Yale
    B. Princeton
    C. William and Mary
    D. Harvard

15. In 1960, how many persons made *Time* magazine's Man of the Year?

    A. 5
    B. 9
    C. 11
    D. 15

ANSWERS ◆ TO $1,000,000 CHALLENGE #16

1. B. *52*
2. D. *Skiffle (a cross between folk and Dixieland music)*
3. A. *Virgil*
4. A. *Joe*
5. C. *Texas*
6. C. *Urceolate*
7. B. *1 (Jan. 1, 1982, Washington over Iowa, 28 to 0)*
8. A. *Roy Hinkley*
9. D. *Pertaining to breakfast*
10. D. *31*
11. A. *Pediatrics*
12. A. *Orson Bean*
13. C. *7 (though he never won)*
14. C. *William and Mary*
15. D. *15 (U.S. scientists, including Edward Teller and Linus Pauling)*

$1,000,000 CHALLENGE 17

1. Which president installed an electric horse in his White House bedroom and rode it regularly?

   A. Coolidge **B.** Harding
   C. Hoover **D.** L. B. J.

2. About how many times does a whale's heart beat per minute?

   A. 9 **B.** 15
   C. 20 **D.** 25

3. In 1931, who invented the electric dry shaver?

   A. Lee Remington **B.** King Camp Gillette
   C. Jacob Schick **D.** Roy Wilkerson

4. How many teeth did George Washington have when he became president?

   A. 1 **B.** 4
   C. 5 **D.** 6

5. What is Evel Knievel's real first name?

   A. Thomas **B.** David
   C. Richard **D.** Robert

6. What is the only state whose five-number zip code consists of the same single numeral?

A. Ohio | **B.** California
C. Alaska | **D.** Hawaii

7. About how much would a million dollars in one-hundred-dollar bills weigh?

A. 20 lbs. | **B.** 25 lbs.
C. 30 lbs. | **D.** 35 lbs.

8. According to the famous Abbott and Costello baseball routine, who played the position of catcher?

A. Because | **B.** Why
C. Tomorrow | **D.** Today

9. How far apart are adjacent bowling pins?

A. 10 inches | **B.** 12 inches
C. 15 inches | **D.** 20 inches

10. Who was the player who was the model for the NBA's silhouette logo?

A. John Havlicek | **B.** George Mikan
C. Bob Cousy | **D.** Jerry West

11. Which of Beethoven's symphonies was on the record player at the Bates Motel in the original *Psycho*?

A. Third | **B.** Fifth
C. Sixth | **D.** Ninth

12. About how many people were in the stands in Mudville that day Mighty Casey struck out?

A. 2000 **B.** 3000
C. 4000 **D.** 5000

13. In which Marx Brothers movie did Margaret Dumont *not* appear?

A. *Animal Crackers* **B.** *The Big Store*
C. *Go West* **D.** *At The Circus*

14. From what pet did John "Duke" Wayne get his nickname?

A. Airedale **B.** German shepherd
C. Schnauzer **D.** Doberman pinscher

15. How many medals were awarded to Audie Murphy, the most highly decorated American soldier in the Second World War?

A. 10 **B.** 11
C. 12 **D.** 15

ANSWERS ◆ TO $1,000,000 CHALLENGE #17

1. A. *Coolidge*
2. A. *9*
3. C. *Jacob Schick*
4. A. *1*
5. D. *Robert (Craig Knievel)*
6. A. *Ohio (Newton Falls, 44444)*
7. A. *20 lbs.*
8. D. *Today*
9. B. *12 inches*
10. D. *Jerry West*
11. A. *Third*
12. D. *5000 (Ten thousand eyes were on him.)*
13. C. *Go West*
14. A. *Airedale*
15. D. *15*

$1,000,000 CHALLENGE 18

1. Who directed the first episode of *Columbo*?

   A. Martin Scorcese **B.** Steven Spielberg
   C. Mike Nichols **D.** George Lucas

2. Where was Jerry Springer born?

   A. Cincinnati, Ohio **B.** Paris, France
   C. Los Angeles, California **D.** London, England

3. What beauty title did Oprah Winfrey win during her college days?

   A. Miss Tennessee **B.** Miss Mississippi
   C. Miss Alabama **D.** Miss Georgia

4. In what year were all but one Nobel Prize given to Americans?

   A. 1969 **B.** 1972
   C. 1975 **D.** 1976

5. In what year did Gary Becker win the Nobel Prize for Economics?

   A. 1992 **B.** 1993
   C. 1994 **D.** 1996

6. For which film did Grace Kelly win an Oscar?

A. *High Noon* **B.** *Dial M for Murder*
C. *To Catch a Thief* **D.** *The Country Girl*

7. Who was the original voice of the Jolly Green Giant, whose only words were "Ho-Ho-Ho"?

A. Hershel Bernardi **B.** Theodore Bikel
C. Alan Reed **D.** William Conrad

8. Which manufacturer originally made the fighter F14 (*Tomcat*)?

A. Northrop **B.** McDonnell-Douglas
C. Grumman **D.** Lockheed

9. What boat did John F. Kennedy command before PT 109?

A. PT 59 **B.** PT 69
C. PT 101 **D.** PT 129

10. What color were Scarlet O'Hara's eyes, according to Margaret Mitchell's *Gone With the Wind*?

A. Blue **B.** Brown
C. Hazel **D.** Green

11. Who was born on exactly the same day as Abraham Lincoln?

A. Charles Darwin **B.** Edward Fitzgerald
C. Edgar Allan Poe **D.** Alfred Lord Tennyson

12. Which playing cards were held by Wild Bill Hickok when he was killed by Jack McCall in 1876?

    A. Black aces and eights
    B. Black kings and nines
    C. Black queens and nines
    D. Black aces and tens

13. On *The Andy Griffith Show*, what was Barney Fife's middle name?

    A. Steven
    B. Bradley
    C. Robert
    D. Oliver

14. Which American president is buried in the same cemetery as John Dillinger, America's first Public Enemy Number One?

    A. Rutherford Hayes
    B. Benjamin Harrison
    C. James Garfield
    D. Warren Harding

15. Of what university was Dwight Eisenhower the president?

    A. Princeton
    B. Yale
    C. Harvard
    D. Columbia

ANSWERS ◆ TO $1,000,000 CHALLENGE #18

1. B. *Steven Spielberg*
2. D. *London, England*
3. A. *Miss Tennessee*
4. D. *1976*
5. A. *1992*
6. D. The Country Girl
7. A. *Hershel Bernardi*
8. C. *Grumman*
9. C. *PT 101*
10. D. Green
11. A. *Charles Darwin*
12. A. *Black aces and eights*
13. D. Oliver
14. B. *Benjamin Harrison*
15. D. Columbia

$1,000,000 CHALLENGE 19

1. What was the original name for the *Today Show*?

   A. *Today*
   B. *The Good Morning Show*
   C. *The Rise and Shine Revue*
   D. *Top of the Morning*

2. According to the Bible, how old was Methuselah's father, Enoch, when Enoch died?

   A. 365
   B. 495
   C. 669
   D. 939

3. Who appeared on the cover of the last edition of *Collier's* magazine on January 4, 1957?

   A. Humphrey Bogart
   B. Grace Kelly
   C. Doris Day
   D. Queen Elizabeth II

4. What was President John F. Kennedy's secret service code name?

   A. Lark
   B. Dapper
   C. Dasher
   D. Lancer

5. What is the pH value of grapefruit?

   A. 5
   B. 4
   C. 3
   D. 2

6. From what state was the license plate on Marion Crane's 1955 Ford in the movie *Psycho*?

A. Colorado | **B.** Arizona
C. New Mexico | **D.** California

7. What state is ranked twenty-sixth in area?

A. Iowa | **B.** Arkansas
C. Illinois | **D.** Wisconsin

8. What sort of star is a type A star?

A. White | **B.** Orange
C. Yellow | **D.** Blue-white

9. According to the Second World War radio usage, what word represented the letter *e*?

A. Echo | **B.** Easy
C. Egg | **D.** East

10. According to the Bible, how many stones did David take with him to face Goliath?

A. 4 | **B.** 5
C. 7 | **D.** 9

11. In order of presidential succession, who would become president after the Secretary of the Interior?

A. Secretary of Commerce | **B.** Secretary of Labor
C. Secretary of Agriculture | **D.** Secretary of Health and Human Services

12. When did Dr. Christian Barnard perform the first successful heart transplant?

A. 1967 **B.** 1966
C. 1965 **D.** 1964

13. In which circle of Hell did the poet Dante place heretics?

A. 3rd **B.** 4th
C. 5th **D.** 6th

14. According to the Library of Congress classification, what letter represents books on language and literature?

A. G **B.** N
C. L **D.** P

15. In Aldous Huxley's novel *Brave New World*, what color do the members of the order gamma wear?

A. Mulberry **B.** Green
C. Gray **D.** Khaki

ANSWERS ◆ TO $1,000,000 CHALLENGE #19

1. C. The Rise and Shine Revue
2. A. *365*
3. B. *Grace Kelly*
4. D. *Lancer*
5. C. *3*
6. B. *Arizona*
7. A. *Iowa*
8. D. *Blue-white (the third youngest and hottest)*
9. B. *Easy*
10. B. *5 (I Samuel 17:40)*
11. C. *Secretary of Agriculture*
12. A. *1967 (Dec. 3)*
13. D. *6th*
14. D. *P*
15. B. *Green*

$1,000,000 CHALLENGE 20

1. What sort of wood are bowling pins made of?

   A. Oak
   B. Maple
   C. Elm
   D. Beech

2. Which philosopher asserted that the goal of philosophy should be to show the fly the way out of the fly bottle?

   A. Ludwig Wittgenstein
   B. J. L. Austin
   C. G. E. Moore
   D. Gilbert Ryle

3. How many pounds of butter are in a firkin?

   A. 12
   B. 24
   C. 30
   D. 56

4. On the day Robert F. Kennedy was shot, what was the number-one pop single in the U.S.?

   A. *This Guy's in Love With You* (Herb Albert)
   B. *MacArthur Park* (Richard Harris)
   C. *Mrs. Robinson* (Simon & Garfunkel)
   D. *Yummy, Yummy, Yummy* (Ohio Express)

5. In the 1976 movie *Ode to Billie Joe*, what did Billie Joe McAllister throw off the Tallahatchee Bridge?

   A. A ring
   B. A diary
   C. A rag doll
   D. A baby

6. About how many pounds of raisins are in a frail?

   A. 18
   B. 24
   C. 36
   D. 75

7. Which fish is the next to the fastest fish of all fish?

   A. Marlin
   B. Sailfish
   C. Bluefin tuna
   D. Yellowfin tuna

8. Which human rib is the longest?

   A. Eighth
   B. Seventh
   C. Sixth
   D. Fifth

9. Of the following types of stars, which one is the hottest?

   A. B
   B. F
   C. O
   D. S

10. What is the middle name of Robert MacNamara, former secretary of defense?

    A. Scanlon
    B. Styles
    C. Shamus
    D. Strange

11. According to a 1997 survey of the National Center for Health Statistics, which U.S. city's population has the next to the largest percentage of obese people?

A. Kansas City, Kansas
B. Norfolk, Virginia
C. New Orleans, Louisiana
D. San Antonio, Texas

12. How many bones are in a human head?

A. 8
B. 7
C. 6
D. 5

13. Which of the following ancient people did *not* speak a Semitic language?

A. Assyrians
B. Phoenicians
C. Sumerians
D. Babylonians

14. Where are the pisiform, lunate, and naviculate bones?

A. Palms
B. Toes
C. Ankles
D. Wrists

15. What king of England was supposed to have made the following remark: "No earthly power can justly call me, who am your king, in question as a delinquent"?

A. Charles I
B. Henry VIII
C. Charles II
D. Henry II

ANSWERS ◆ TO $1,000,000 CHALLENGE #20

1. B. *Maple*
2. A. *Ludwig Wittgenstein*
3. D. *56*
4. C. *Mrs. Robinson*
5. C. *A rag doll*
6. D. *75*
7. A. *Martin*
8. B. *Seventh*
9. C. *O*
10. D. *Strange*
11. B. *Norfolk, Virginia*
12. A. *8*
13. C. *Sumerians*
14. D. *Wrists*
15. A. *Charles I*

$1,000,000 CHALLENGE 21

1. According to estimates of the U.S. Bureau of the Census/United Nations for the year 2000, what country qualified as the third most densely populated in the world?

   A. Singapore
   B. Bahrain
   C. Malta
   D. Bangladesh

2. How many consecutive basketball games were won by the UCLA Bruins between January 24, 1971, and January 29, 1974?

   A. 74
   B. 78
   C. 84
   D. 88

3. Which magazine was established first?

   A. *Town & Country*
   B. *Harper's*
   C. *Scientific American*
   D. *The Atlantic*

4. Which of the following trees has the most streets named after it in the U.S., according to the U.S. Bureau of the Census?

   A. Elm
   B. Maple
   C. Pine
   D. Oak

5. In what year was the comic book hero the Human Torch introduced in Marvel Comics?

   A. 1938
   B. 1939
   C. 1940
   D. 1941

6. Next to The Beatles, which music artist sold the most albums in the U.S. as of January 1, 2000?

A. Garth Brooks
B. Elvis Presley
C. Billy Joel
D. Barbra Streisand

7. In what year was the Toyota Corolla introduced?

A. 1966
B. 1967
C. 1968
D. 1969

8. When actor Laurence Fishburne was nine years old, on what soap opera did he appear regularly?

A. *As the World Turns*
B. *The Young and the Restless*
C. *Days of our Lives*
D. *One Life to Live*

9. What car has been the best-selling car of all time?

A. Ford Model T
B. Honda Civic
C. Toyota Corolla
D. Volkswagen Beetle

10. How many persons, of the 97 on board the *Hindenburg* airship, survived?

A. 71
B. 61
C. 31
D. 21

11. With what team was Burt Reynolds signed to play football?

A. Baltimore Colts
B. Oakland Raiders
C. New York Jets
D. Detroit Lions

12. What country consumes the most sugar per capita according to the Food and Agriculture Organization of the United Nations?

    A. Cuba　　**B.** Belize
    C. Israel　　**D.** Barbados

13. Of what state was actress Jane Seymour named an honorary citizen in 1977?

    A. Michigan　　**B.** Illinois
    C. Indiana　　**D.** Wisconsin

14. What is the number of Vietnam's Hamburger Hill?

    A. 937　　**B.** 837
    C. 737　　**D.** 637

15. From 1970 through 1978, how many years were there in which two college football teams became national champions because of a disagreement between UPI and AP polls?

    A. 4　　**B.** 3
    C. 2　　**D.** 1

ANSWERS ◆ TO $1,000,000 CHALLENGE #21

1. C. *Malta*
2. D. *88*
3. C. Scientific American *(1845)*
4. D. *Oak*
5. C. *1940*
6. A. *Garth Brooks (92,000,000)*
7. A. *1966*
8. D. One Life to Live
9. C. *Toyota Corolla (about 23 million were sold as of the year 2000)*
10. B. *61*
11. A. *Baltimore Colts*
12. C. *Israel*
13. B. *Illinois*
14. A. *937*
15. A. *4*

$1,000,000 CHALLENGE 22

1. In the Mother Goose rhyme ("Here We Go Round the Mulberry Bush"), when do "we mend our clothes"?

   A. "So early Thursday morning" **B.** "So early Friday morning"
   C. "So early Saturday morning" **D.** "So early Sunday morning"

2. How much money did Elvis Presley first receive from the U.S. for his monthly salary?

   A. $65.20 **B.** $83.20
   C. $91.20 **D.** $93.20

3. What was the first name of Lana Turner's daughter accused of stabbing to death Johnny Stompanato?

   A. Sheri **B.** Cheryl
   C. Sheila **D.** Sheena

4. How old was Admiral Hyman Rickover when President Reagan ordered him to step down from his post?

   A. 77 **B.** 78
   C. 80 **D.** 81

5. What is a specific name for a group of eagles?

A. Convocation
B. Congregation
C. Covey
D. Exaltation

6. Whom did comic book hero Superman fight in February 1976 when DC Comics and Marvel Comics collaborated?

A. Muhammad Ali
B. Batman
C. The Amazing Spider-Man
D. The Thing

7. What was the first name of the artist who painted the picture of Dorian Gray in Oscar Wilde's novel of that name?

A. Geoffrey
B. Robert
C. Gerald
D. Basil

8. In what year did tennis player Bobby Riggs sweep Wimbledon?

A. 1938
B. 1939
C. 1940
D. 1941

9. A letter to what newspaper sparked the response that began "Yes, Virginia, there is a Santa Claus"?

A. *New York Sun*
B. *New York Times*
C. *Chicago Sun*
D. *Atlanta Constitution*

10. What was the name of Lizzie Borden's father?

A. Michael
B. Robert
C. Andrew
D. James

11. From what state was the first woman elected to the U.S. Senate?

A. New York | **B.** Massachusetts
C. Wyoming | **D.** Arkansas

12. Who was the first American president to visit a foreign country while in office?

A. Theodore Roosevelt | **B.** William H. Taft
C. Woodrow Wilson | **D.** Calvin Coolidge

13. In January 1972, which soft drink was pulled from the shelves because some of the aluminum lids on the cans were contaminated?

A. Pepsi | **B.** Coca-Cola
C. Dr Pepper | **D.** 7 Up

14. What is the name of the first woman to take part in the Oxford-Cambridge boat race?

A. Margaret White | **B.** Mary Smith
C. Susan Brown | **D.** Marsha White

15. What is the only planet in our solar system that rotates clockwise?

A. Mercury | **B.** Mars
C. Venus | **D.** Pluto

ANSWERS ◆ TO $1,000,000 CHALLENGE #22

1. A. *"So early Thursday morning"*
2. B. *$83.20*
3. B. *Cheryl (Crane)*
4. D. *81*
5. A. *Convocation*
6. C. *The Amazing Spider-Man*
7. D. *Basil (Hallward)*
8. B. *1939*
9. A. New York Sun
10. C. *Andrew*
11. D. *Arkansas (Hattie Caraway)*
12. A. *Theodore Roosevelt (Panama)*
13. B. *Coca-Cola*
14. C. *Susan Brown (in 1981)*
15. C. *Venus*

$1,000,000 CHALLENGE 23

1. According to *Entertainment Weekly*, who was Entertainer of the Year, 1999?

   A. Britney Spears
   B. Ricky Martin
   C. Julia Roberts
   D. Regis Philbin

2. What is the name of the first asteroid to be discovered?

   A. Ceres
   B. Pallas
   C. Juno
   D. Vesta

3. Who was originally supposed to play district attorney Hamilton Burger in the TV Show *Perry Mason*?

   A. Jack Klugman
   B. John Forsythe
   C. Raymond Burr
   D. Robert Cummings

4. How many nominations did *The Sopranos* receive in the 1999–2000 Emmy Awards?

   A. 11
   B. 13
   C. 15
   D. 16

5. In what year did Joe DiMaggio's 56-game hitting streak come to an end?

   A. 1940
   B. 1941
   C. 1942
   D. 1943

6. For what sport is the Borg-Warner trophy given?

A. Auto racing
B. Soccer
C. Hockey
D. Miniature golf

7. Which one of the following singers was the youngest of the four to have a number-one single in the U.S.?

A. Leslie Gore
B. Britney Spears
C. Brenda Lee
D. Monica

8. What is the oldest U.S. bridge in continuous use?

A. Haverhill Bath Bridge (Bath/Haverhill, New Hampshire)
B. Brooklyn Bridge (Brooklyn/Manhattan)
C. Cape Cod Canal Bridge (Cape Cod, Massachusetts)
D. Frankford Avenue Bridge (Philadelphia)

9. In what year was the soft drink Sprite introduced?

A. 1961
B. 1962
C. 1963
D. 1964

10. What month is Aviation History Month and International Drum Month?

A. April
B. June
C. September
D. November

11. Who was the oldest female singer to have a number-one single in the U.S.?

A. Bette Midler
B. Cher
C. Kim Carnes
D. Tina Turner

12. According to the National Center for Health Statistics, which U.S. city has the smallest percentage of obese people?

A. Minneapolis, Minnesota **B.** San Diego, California
C. Denver, Colorado **D.** Washington, D.C.

13. Which is the largest NFL stadium?

A. Arrowhead Stadium **B.** Giants Stadium
C. Pontiac Silverdome **D.** Pro Player Stadium

14. In what century did Thomas Hobson, who hired out horses in strict rotation at Cambridge University and who gave us the expression "Hobson's choice," die?

A. Sixteenth **B.** Seventeenth
C. Eighteenth **D.** Nineteenth

15. What modern baseball pitcher holds the record for the most wins in one year?

A. Jack Chesbro **B.** Christy Mathewson
C. Cy Young **D.** Joe McGinnity

ANSWERS ◆ TO $1,000,000 CHALLENGE #23

1. B. *Ricky Martin*
2. A. *Ceres*
3. C. *Raymond Burr*
4. D. *16 (won 4)*
5. B. *1941 (when he went 0 for 3 against the Cleveland Indians on July 17)*
6. A. *Auto racing (the Indianapolis 500)*
7. C. *Brenda Lee ("I'm Sorry," in 1960, at 15 years, 7 months, 7 days)*
8. D. *Frankford Avenue Bridge (1697)*
9. A. *1961*
10. D. *November*
11. D. *Tina Turner ("Believe," in 1999, at 52 years, 9 months, 15 days)*
12. C. *Denver, Colorado*
13. C. *Pontiac Silverdome*
14. B. *Seventeenth (1544?–1631)*
15. A. *Jack Chesbro*

$1,000,000 CHALLENGE 24

1. What does the Knoop scale measure?

   A. The hardness of minerals
   B. The resilience of bridges
   C. The wind-chill factor
   D. Psychological stress

2. In the measurement of alcohol, how many shots make a pint?

   A. 4
   B. 8
   C. 12
   D. 16

3. Which was first?

   A. *Mad* magazine
   B. *TV Guide*
   C. The marriage of Marilyn Monroe and Joe DiMaggio
   D. Ann Landers's column in the *Chicago Sun-Times*

4. Who provided the voice of Johnny Storm, the Human Torch, on Marvel Comics' radio show *The Fantastic Four*?

   A. Dan Aykroyd
   B. Bill Murray
   C. Chevy Chase
   D. Bill Mahr

5. What was the first record the Beatles released that entered the British charts?

   A. "I Want to Hold Your Hand"
   B. "She Loves You"
   C. "Love Me Do"
   D. "Please Please Me"

6. Which did *not* occur in 1956?

   A. Grace Kelly marries Prince Monroe Rainier III of Monaco.

   B. Jerry Lewis and Dean Martin split.

   C. Leonard Bernstein is named the first American musical director of the New York Philharmonic.

   D. Marilyn Monroe marries Arthur Miller.

7. For a 68-week period that began August 8, 1963, who was the only American recording artist to have a number-one single in Britain?

   A. Roy Orbison

   B. Wayne Newton

   C. Elvis Presley

   D. Bobby Vinton

8. Who did *not* die in 1965?

   A. T. S. Eliot

   B. Clara Bow

   C. Buster Keaton

   D. Winston Churchill

9. What was the original title of Paul McCartney's "Yesterday"?

   A. "Scrambled Eggs"

   B. "Rotten Eggs"

   C. "Painful Memories"

   D. "It Was Better Then"

10. On what birthday did Madonna marry Sean Penn?

    A. Her twenty-fifth

    B. Her twenty-eighth

    C. Her thirtieth

    D. Her thirty-second

11. What artist's painting hung upside down between October 18 and December 4, 1961, in New York's Museum of Modern Art?

    A. Klee's

    B. Picasso's

    C. Pollock's

    D. Matisse's

12. Who lived at 448 Bonnie Meadow Road?

A. Darrin Stephens and his family **B.** Rob Petrie and his family
C. Andy Taylor and his family **D.** Ward Cleaver and his family

13. What was Jerry Mathers's first acting role?

A. A character in the TV show *Leave It to Beaver*
B. A character in the movie *The Man Who Knew Too Much*
C. A character in the movie *The Trouble With Harry*
D. A character in *Davy Crockett and the River Pirates*

14. What number iron was used by astronaut Alan Shepard to hit three golf balls on the moon on February 6, 1971?

A. Two iron **B.** Three iron
C. Five iron **D.** Six iron

15. When was Halley's comet last observed?

A. 1996 **B.** 1986
C. 1976 **D.** 1966

ANSWERS ◆ TO $1,000,000 CHALLENGE #24

1. A. The hardness of minerals
2. D. 16
3. A. Mad magazine (1952)
4. B. Bill Murray
5. C. "Love Me Do"
6. C. Leonard Bernstein is named the first American musical director of the New York Philharmonic (1957)
7. A. Roy Orbison
8. C. Buster Keaton (1966)
9. A. "Scrambled Eggs"
10. A. Her twenty-fifth
11. D. Matisse's (Le Bateau)
12. B. Rob Petrie and his family
13. C. A character in the movie The Trouble With Harry
14. D. Six iron
15. B. 1986

$1,000,000 CHALLENGE 25

1. What is Barbie doll's middle name?

   A. Anne
   B. Ilene
   C. Fae
   D. Millicent

2. In cooking, how many drops are in a thimbleful?

   A. 10
   B. 20
   C. 30
   D. 35

3. Which U.S. state ranked first in rates for public high school graduation during the 1997–1998 school year?

   A. Iowa
   B. North Dakota
   C. Nebraska
   D. Minnesota

4. In what state was Theodore Roosevelt shot and wounded on October 14, 1912?

   A. New York
   B. Illinois
   C. Wisconsin
   D. Pennsylvania

5. In March 1969, for how long was James Earl Ray sentenced for the crime of killing Martin Luther King, Jr.?

   A. 99 years
   B. 120 years
   C. 3 consecutive life sentences
   D. 4 consecutive life sentences

6. Which letter is the most frequently used in our alphabet?

A. A
B. E
C. I
D. O

7. Which American president's wife was the first to be called the first lady?

A. Dolley Madison
B. Louisa Catherine Johnson Adams
C. Julia Gardiner Tyler
D. Lucy Ware Webb Hayes

8. In 1939, where did the fad of goldfish-swallowing begin?

A. Harvard University
B. Yale University
C. Princeton University
D. Dartmouth University

9. About how many years did it take Leonardo da Vinci to paint the *Mona Lisa*?

A. 3
B. 4
C. 5
D. 6

10. What does the *K* represent in newscaster Howard K. Smith's name?

A. Kingsbury
B. Kent
C. Keith
D. Kelly

11. What woman held the Miss America title for two consecutive years?

A. Bette Cooper
B. Henrietta Leaver
C. Mary Campbell
D. Barbara Walker

12. Which of the following countries does *not* have red in its flag?

    A. Zambia **B.** Guyana
    C. Mauritania **D.** Mauritius

13. What movie did Spielberg direct the earliest?

    A. *The Sugarland Express* **B.** *Duel*
    C. *Close Encounters of the Third Kind* **D.** *Jaws*

14. In what month is Independence Day in Nigeria?

    A. September **B.** October
    C. November **D.** December

15. In what year did Barbara Jordan first win a seat in the Texas senate?

    A. 1963 **B.** 1964
    C. 1965 **D.** 1966

ANSWERS ◆ TO $1,000,000 CHALLENGE #25

1. D. *Millicent*
2. C. *30*
3. A. *Iowa (with its 88.7 percent rate)*
4. C. *Wisconsin*
5. A. *99 years*
6. B. *E*
7. D. *Lucy Ware Webb Hayes*
8. A. *Harvard University*
9. B. *4 (1503–1507)*
10. A. *Kingsbury*
11. C. *Mary Campbell*
12. C. *Mauritania (whose flag is yellow on green)*
13. B. Duel
14. B. *October (October 1, 1960)*
15. D. *1966*

$1,000,000 CHALLENGE 26

1. About how long is a cosmic year?

   A. 75 million Earth years
   B. 125 million Earth years
   C. 150 million Earth years
   D. 225 million Earth years

2. Which actor played the villain in the pilot for the *Batman* television series?

   A. Burgess Meredith
   B. Frank Gorshin
   C. John Astin
   D. Caesar Romero

3. In what year was baseball's World Series launched?

   A. 1903
   B. 1906
   C. 1908
   D. 1909

4. Which came first?

   A. The building of the first drive-in movie theater
   B. The movie *Becky Sharp*
   C. The death of John Dillinger
   D. The winning of four Olympic gold medals in track by Jesse Owens

5. How many completed *Canterbury Tales* are there?

   A. 12
   B. 18
   C. 24
   D. 32

6. In the year 2000, what was the yearly income for the Majority Leader of the U.S. Senate?

   A. $125,000 **B.** $132,000
   C. $141,300 **D.** $157,000

7. What was the real middle name of British author George Orwell?

   A. Russell **B.** Arthur
   C. Stanley **D.** Stephen

8. In what country did Sherlock Holmes's rival Moriarty die?

   A. Switzerland **B.** France
   C. England **D.** Italy

9. How wide is a golf hole?

   A. 4 inches **B.** 4.25 inches
   C. 4.5 inches **D.** 4.75 inches

10. How many peanuts per ounce are in each box of Cracker Jacks?

    A. 6 **B.** 7
    C. 8 **D.** 9

11. For how many years must people have been U.S. citizens before they are eligible for the U.S. Senate?

    A. 4 **B.** 5
    C. 7 **D.** 9

12. Who was president when running water was installed in the White House?

A. John Quincy Adams
B. Andrew Jackson
C. Martin Van Buren
D. William Henry Harrison

13. Who is the Christian patron saint of the insane?

A. Dymphna
B. Benedict
C. Mathurin
D. Jude

14. To which sect or school did philosophers Parmenides and Melissus belong?

A. Cyrenaic
B. Ionic
C. Eleatic
D. Megaric

15. How many times was the British Open won by Tom Watson?

A. 2
B. 3
C. 4
D. 5

ANSWERS ◆ TO $1,000,000 CHALLENGE #26

1. D. *225 million Earth years (the time it takes the sun to complete one revolution around the center of the Milky Way galaxy)*
2. B. *Frank Gorshin*
3. A. *1903*
4. A. *The building of the first drive-in theater (in 1933 in Camden, New Jersey)*
5. C. *24*
6. D. *$157,000*
7. B. *Arthur (Eric Arthur Blair)*
8. A. *Switzerland*
9. B. *4.25 inches*
10. D. *9*
11. D. *9*
12. B. *Andrew Jackson*
13. A. *Dymphna*
14. C. *Eleatic*
15. D. *5*

$1,000,000 CHALLENGE 27

1. In 1999, which company spent the most on advertising?

   A. General Motors
   B. Procter & Gamble
   C. Philip Morris
   D. Time Warner

2. Which politician was born first?

   A. Dick Cheney
   B. William Cohen
   C. Dianne Feinstein
   D. Thomas Daschle

3. What element is number 109 on the periodic table?

   A. Hahnium
   B. Hassium
   C. Bohrium
   D. Meitnerium

4. In the American Film Institute's list of the 100 Best American Movies of All Time, which movie is in the list but not mentioned within the first ten?

   A. *It's a Wonderful Life*
   B. *Schindler's List*
   C. *Singin' in the Rain*
   D. *The Graduate*

5. How much was the first U.S. minimum wage per hour?

   A. 25¢
   B. 35¢
   C. 50¢
   D. 75¢

6. Of the following astronauts, who spent the most time on the moon's surface outside the lunar module?

   A. John W. Young
   B. James B. Irwin
   C. David R. Scott
   D. Edgar D. Mitchell

7. According to the National Climatic Data Center, which of the following is *not* one of the 10 wettest American cities?

   A. West Palm Beach, Florida
   B. Tallahassee, Florida
   C. Seattle, Washington
   D. Mobile, Alabama

8. What moon/satellite is the next to the largest in our solar system?

   A. Ganymede
   B. Titan
   C. Io
   D. Europa

9. In how many of his 153 movies did John Wayne *not* have a leading role?

   A. 11
   B. 12
   C. 13
   D. 14

10. Who wrote "Oh what a tangled web we weave when first we practice to deceive"?

    A. Robert Burns
    B. Robert Southey
    C. Sir Walter Scott
    D. Alexander Pope

11. Who was ABC's first choice for the role of Mr. Roarke in *Fantasy Island*?

    A. Robert Vaughn
    B. Orson Welles
    C. Jack Lord
    D. Robert Reed

12. From what author did American physicist Murray Gell-Mann derive the word *quark*?

    A. Edward Lear　　**B.** Lewis Carroll
    C. Hilaire Belloc　　**D.** James Joyce

13. What word in Hinduism is roughly translated as "earthly gain"?

    A. *Kama*　　**B.** *Artha*
    C. *Dharma*　　**D.** *Moksha*

14. In the 1855 first edition of *Bartlett's Familiar Quotations*, how many people quoted were women?

    A. 2　　**B.** 4
    C. 6　　**D.** 8

15. In which circle of Dante's Hell/Inferno are betrayers of their family or country (such as Judas) frozen in ice?

    A. Sixth　　**B.** Seventh
    C. Eighth　　**D.** Ninth

ANSWERS ◆ TO $1,000,000 CHALLENGE #27

1. A. *General Motors*
2. C. *Dianne Feinstein*
3. D. *Meitnerium (also known as unnilennium)*
4. A. It's a Wonderful Life *(which is number 11)*
5. A. *25¢*
6. A. *John W. Young (20 hours and 14 minutes)*
7. C. *Seattle, Washington (though Quillayute, Washington, is first on the list)*
8. B. *Titan (a moon of Saturn)*
9. A. *11*
10. C. *Sir Walter Scott*
11. B. *Orson Welles*
12. D. *James Joyce* (Finnegans Wake)
13. B. Artha
14. B. *4*
15. D. *Ninth*

$1,000,000 CHALLENGE 28

1. How much money did Norman Lear and David Hayden pay for one of the surviving copies of the Declaration of Independence?

   A. $4.7 million **B.** $5.2 million
   C. $6.5 million **D.** $7.4 million

2. As of October 2000, which state's governor earned $65,000 as a yearly salary?

   A. Arkansas **B.** Nebraska
   C. West Virginia **D.** North Dakota

3. Which entertainer's original name was Jacob Cohen?

   A. Rodney Dangerfield **B.** Howard Cosell
   C. Mel Brooks **D.** Phil Silvers

4. According to the opinions of the editors of *World Almanac 2001*, which star was *not* among the top-ten favorite stars of all time?

   A. Grace Kelly **B.** Audrey Hepburn
   C. Jim Carrey **D.** Ingrid Bergman

5. As of the year 2000, which female musical artist had won the most Grammys?

   A. Madonna **B.** Barbra Streisand
   C. Whitney Houston **D.** Aretha Franklin

6. Which flower has been most closely associated with Japanese royalty?

   A. Orchid | **B.** Maple
   C. Chrysanthemum | **D.** Orange Blossom

7. Which Japanese city was not chosen for the dropping of the atomic bomb because of weather?

   A. Kokura | **B.** Kyoto
   C. Tokyo | **D.** Kagoshima

8. What word is roughly synonymous with "gentleness"?

   A. Desuetude | **B.** Mansuetude
   C. Consuetude | **D.** Assuetude

9. How many regular vetoes did Grover Cleveland use in his first term?

   A. 186 | **B.** 205
   C. 264 | **D.** 304

10. Which state contains counties named after William McKinley, Theodore Roosevelt, and Warren G. Harding?

    A. New Mexico | **B.** Arizona
    C. Wyoming | **D.** Massachusetts

11. According to the Bureau of the Census, which U.S. state in 1998 had the largest number of American Indians?

    A. Oklahoma | **B.** Arizona
    C. California | **D.** New Mexico

12. Where was the home of the winning team in the 2000 Little League World Series?

    A. Venezuela
    B. Japan
    C. Taiwan
    D. Mexico

13. Who was the last golfer before Tiger Woods to win three major championships in one year?

    A. Jack Nicklaus
    B. Gary Player
    C. Arnold Palmer
    D. Ben Hogan

14. Who was on the first U.S. commemorative coin?

    A. George Washington
    B. Christopher Columbus
    C. Abraham Lincoln
    D. Patrick Henry

15. Who was the last American president *not* to have a single library dedicated to his papers?

    A. William McKinley
    B. Warren Harding
    C. Calvin Coolidge
    D. Herbert Hoover

ANSWERS ◆ TO $1,000,000 CHALLENGE #28

1. D. *$7.4 million*
2. B. *Nebraska*
3. A. *Rodney Dangerfield*
4. C. *Jim Carrey*
5. D. *Aretha Franklin*
6. C. *Chrysanthemum*
7. A. *Kokura*
8. B. *Mansuetude*
9. D. *304*
10. A. *New Mexico*
11. C. *California*
12. A. *Venezuela*
13. D. *Ben Hogan (in 1953)*
14. B. *Christopher Columbus (in 1892)*
15. C. *Calvin Coolidge*

$1,000,000 CHALLENGE 29

1. At what university did a computer malfunction in 1945 because of a moth, giving us the expression "computer bug"?

   A. Princeton **B.** Yale
   C. M.I.T. **D.** Harvard

2. How long was the Monday Night Football game played between the New York Jets and the Miami Dolphins on October 23, 2000?

   A. 3 hours, 10 minutes **B.** 3 hours, 20 minutes
   C. 4 hours, 10 minutes **D.** 4 hours, 20 minutes

3. What game was first called mintonette?

   A. Volleyball **B.** Badminton
   C. Tennis **D.** Croquet

4. What was the first name of Grandpa Walton on the TV show *The Waltons*?

   A. Zeke **B.** Jonas
   C. Zeb **D.** Caleb

5. How many spots were painted on each Dalmatian puppy in Disney's animated film *101 Dalmatians*?

   A. 22 **B.** 32
   C. 66 **D.** 77

6. What was the original name of the washing machine, invented by Alvin Fisher?

A. Thor **B.** Poseidon
C. Neptune **D.** Aquarius

7. Who invented barbed wire in the 1870s?

A. Robert Hare **B.** Seth Wheeler
C. James Ritty **D.** Joseph Glidden

8. How many years did England's Queen Victoria reign?

A. 49 **B.** 52
C. 64 **D.** 66

9. What type of tree includes the Formosa incense, Clanwilliam, and Barbados?

A. Cedar **B.** Magnolia
C. Pine **D.** Spruce

10. In what state is the geographic center of the North American continent?

A. Kansas **B.** North Dakota
C. South Dakota **D.** Nebraska

11. What flower includes cobras, soldiers, golden swans, and mirrors?

A. Orchids **B.** Petunias
C. Forget-Me-Nots **D.** Tulips

12. Which event did *not* occur in 1981?

    A. The first U.S. space shuttle, *Columbia*, made its maiden flight.
    B. Robert De Niro won the Best Actor Academy Award.
    C. A Boeing 737 crashed into the Potomac River in Washington, D.C.
    D. The first woman in 542 years was elected a Fellow of All Souls College, Oxford.

13. What does the *S* represent in the acronym THRUSH, the evil society in the TV series *The Man from U.N.C.L.E.*?

    A. Surveillance
    B. Subjugation
    C. Sabotage
    D. Subordination

14. Which U.S. state's name comes from an Indian term meaning "river of the big canoes"?

    A. Nebraska
    B. Mississippi
    C. Michigan
    D. Missouri

15. Of the following people, who has *not* won the Best Actor Academy Award twice?

    A. Marlon Brando
    B. Frederic March
    C. Jack Lemmon
    D. Gary Cooper

ANSWERS ◆ TO $1,000,000 CHALLENGE #29

1. D. *Harvard*
2. C. *4 hours, 10 minutes*
3. A. *Volleyball*
4. C. *Zeb*
5. B. *32*
6. A. *Thor (Norse god of rain and thunder)*
7. D. *Joseph Glidden*
8. C. *64*
9. A. *Cedar*
10. B. *North Dakota (6 miles west of Balta, Pierce County)*
11. A. *Orchids*
12. C. *A Boeing 737 crashed into the Potomac River in Washington, D.C. (happened in 1982)*
13. B. *Subjugation (The Technological Hierarchy for the Removal of Undesirables and the Subjugation of Humanity)*
14. D. *Missouri*
15. C. *Jack Lemmon*

$1,000,000 CHALLENGE 30

1. When it is 11 A.M. in Fargo, North Dakota, what time is it in Honolulu, Hawaii?

   A. 5 A.M. **B.** 6 A.M.
   C. 7 A.M. **D.** 8 A.M.

2. In what year did two people win the Sullivan Award, an award for outstanding amateur athletes?

   A. 1997 **B.** 1998
   C. 1999 **D.** 2000

3. Which word did *not* make language expert Wilfred Funk's list of the ten most beautiful words in English?

   A. Velvet **B.** Dawn
   C. Hush **D.** Chimes

4. In 1998, what was the third most populous American city?

   A. Los Angeles **B.** Chicago
   C. Houston **D.** Philadelphia

5. What was the name of the duck-billed platypus that was one of the three official mascots at the 2000 Olympics in Sydney?

   A. Syd **B.** Millie
   C. Olly **D.** Nosey

6. Where will the 2006 Winter Olympic Games be held?

   A. France
   B. Italy
   C. U.S.
   D. Japan

7. What is the only movie Charles Laughton ever directed?

   A. *The Night of the Hunter*
   B. *The Hunchback of Notre Dame*
   C. *Forever and a Day*
   D. *Hobson's Choice*

8. On the TV sitcom *Night Court*, what was the real first name of the bailiff, Bull Shannon?

   A. Zeus
   B. Odysseus
   C. Jedidiah
   D. Nostradamus

9. Which is the only movie in which the singer Marni Nixon appeared?

   A. *Big City*
   B. *The King and I*
   C. *My Fair Lady*
   D. *The Sound of Music*

10. What do the initials "J. C." stand for in football-player-turned-Congressman J. C. Watts Jr.'s name?

    A. John Carlson
    B. James Carlton
    C. Jesse Charles
    D. Julius Caesar

11. For what newspaper did both Ernest Hemingway and Walt Disney work?

    A. *Kansas City Star*
    B. *The New York Times*
    C. *Phoenix Arizona Republic*
    D. *Los Angeles Times*

12. What activity is *not* part of the modern pentathlon?

A. Running
B. Swimming
C. Discus throwing
D. Pistol shooting

13. What sorts of weapons are dokwera, karakdosura, and shishina?

A. Arrows
B. Swords
C. Knives
D. Spears

14. What is the name of the school newspaper in the TV show *Happy Days*?

A. *Jefferson Crier*
B. *Jefferson Gazette*
C. *Jefferson Star*
D. *Jefferson Pilot*

15. In what movie did Greta Garbo say "I want to be alone"?

A. *As You Desire Me*
B. *Anna Karenina*
C. *The Mysterious Lady*
D. *Grand Hotel*

ANSWERS ◆ TO $1,000,000 CHALLENGE #30

1. C. *7 A.M.*
2. C. 1999 (*Coco and Kelly Miller, basketball players at the University of Georgia*)
3. A. *Velvet*
4. B. *Chicago*
5. A. *Syd*
6. B. *Italy*
7. A. The Night of the Hunter
8. D. *Nostradamus*
9. D. The Sound of Music (*as a nun*)
10. D. *Julius Caesar*
11. A. Kansas City Star
12. C. *Discus throwing*
13. A. *Arrows (used by South American hunter-gatherers)*
14. A. Jefferson Crier
15. D. Grand Hotel

$1,000,000 CHALLENGE 31

1. According to *Entrepreneur* magazine (January 2000), what is the minimum start-up cost (excluding franchise fees) for a 7-Eleven convenience store?

   A. $12,500 **B.** $25,500
   C. $52,500 **D.** $89,500

2. In 1999, which U.S. state had the fewest residents?

   A. North Dakota **B.** Alaska
   C. Vermont **D.** Wyoming

3. How many people, according to official records, were killed by the Great Fire of London in 1666, in which more than 13,000 homes were destroyed?

   A. 6 **B.** 66
   C. 666 **D.** 6,666

4. In 1999, which U.S. state had the highest per capita income of any state?

   A. New Jersey **B.** Connecticut
   C. New York **D.** Colorado

5. Which state is *not* known as the Sunshine State?

A. Florida
B. California
C. New Mexico
D. South Dakota

6. In what year did the U.S. nuclear submarine *Thresher* sink in the Atlantic Ocean?

A. 1963
B. 1964
C. 1965
D. 1966

7. What is the only tribe of American Indians to have inhabited what is now Yellowstone National Park?

A. Cherokee
B. Sioux
C. Shoshone
D. Navajo

8. Where did the wife of King Richard I (Richard the Lion-Hearted) live?

A. England
B. France
C. Germany
D. Italy

9. How many Heisman trophy winners did college football coach Bear Bryant coach?

A. 1
B. 3
C. 4
D. 5

10. How many ballets did George Handel compose?

A. 0
B. 1
C. 2
D. 3

11. How many jockeys have won the Triple Crown twice?

A. 0 **B.** 1
C. 2 **D.** 3

12. Who is the only author to have a U.S. space program site on another planet named for him?

A. Ray Bradbury **B.** Arthur C. Clarke
C. Isaac Asimov **D.** H. G. Wells

13. Which signer of the Declaration of Independence lived the longest?

A. John Adams **B.** Thomas Jefferson
C. William Floyd **D.** Charles Carroll

14. In what U.S. state was volleyball invented?

A. New York **B.** Illinois
C. Massachusetts **D.** California

15. What was the middle name of actor George C. Scott?

A. Charles **B.** Campbell
C. Carson **D.** Conrad

ANSWERS ◆ TO $1,000,000 CHALLENGE #31

1. A. *$12,500*
2. D. *Wyoming*
3. A. *6*
4. B. *Connecticut*
5. B. *California*
6. A. *1963*
7. C. *Shoshone*
8. D. *Italy*
9. A. *1 (John David Crow, a running back who won the trophy when playing for Texas A&M, where Bryant once coached)*
10. B. *1* (A Dramatic Entertainment)
11. B. *1 (Eddie Arcaro rode Whirlaway to the Triple Crown in 1941 and Citation to the Triple Crown in 1948.)*
12. A. *Ray Bradbury*
13. D. *Charles Carroll*
14. C. *Massachusetts*
15. B. *Campbell*

$1,000,000 CHALLENGE 32

1. What crimes does the god Orcus punish?

   A. Theft **B.** Murder
   C. Mayhem **D.** Perjury

2. In what U.S. state will you find Sparks, Nellis, Weed Heights, and Elko?

   A. Nevada **B.** Wyoming
   C. Kansas **D.** North Dakota

3. Who invented the field ion microscope?

   A. Knoll **B.** Ruska
   C. Mueller **D.** Janssen

4. What was the name of Gene Autry's horse?

   A. Cincinnati **B.** Champion
   C. Tony **D.** Stalwart

5. What does the name "Honduras" literally mean?

   A. Depths **B.** Heights
   C. Arroyo **D.** Pit

6. What was named the number-two icon of the 20th century by *Advertising Age* magazine?

   A. The Marlboro Man　　**B.** Jolly Green Giant
   C. Betty Crocker　　**D.** Ronald McDonald

7. How many stars are on the U.S. national flag of 1818?

   A. 13　　**B.** 15
   C. 18　　**D.** 20

8. What is the name of the yellow U.S. flag containing a coiled snake and the words "Don't tread on me"?

   A. Taunton flag　　**B.** Navy Jack
   C. Gadsden flag　　**D.** Continental flag

9. What does the chiefly Scottish word *houder* mean?

   A. To heap or crowd together　　**B.** To separate
   C. To repel　　**D.** To confuse

10. On a ship, where is the orlop deck?

    A. Lowest deck　　**B.** Next to the lowest deck
    C. Middle deck　　**D.** Highest deck

11. Which celebrity's original name is Caryn Johnson?

    A. Whoopi Goldberg　　**B.** Shelley Winters
    C. Wynonna Judd　　**D.** Carole King

12. Where is the Newseum, containing news photography?

A. Los Angeles, California
B. New York, New York
C. Washington, D.C.
D. Arlington, Virginia

13. Judged by the percentage of TV-owning households tuning in, which one of the following Super Bowls was the most popular?

A. Super Bowl XVI
B. Super Bowl XX
C. Super Bowl XXX
D. Super Bowl XXXII

14. Whose original last name is Epstein?

A. Albert Brooks
B. Mel Brooks
C. Kathie Lee Gifford
D. Steve Lawrence

15. In what decade did the Book-of-the-Month Club begin?

A. 1920s
B. 1930s
C. 1940s
D. 1950s

ANSWERS ◆ TO $1,000,000 CHALLENGE #32

1. D. *Perjury*
2. A. *Nevada*
3. C. *Mueller*
4. B. *Champion*
5. A. *Depths*
6. D. *Ronald McDonald (who was second to the Marlboro Man)*
7. D. *20*
8. C. *Gadsden flag*
9. A. *To heap or crowd together*
10. A. *Lowest deck*
11. A. *Whoopi Goldberg*
12. D. *Arlington, Virginia*
13. A. *Super Bowl XVI*
14. C. *Kathie Lee Gifford*
15. A. *1920s (1926)*

$1,000,000 CHALLENGE 33

1. Who received the first gold record?

   A. Xavier Cugat
   B. Paul Whiteman
   C. Tommy Dorsey
   D. Glenn Miller

2. What was the name of the brother and business partner of John Dodge, auto manufacturer?

   A. Robert
   B. Horace
   C. Irving
   D. Samuel

3. In what academic discipline did G. H. Darwin, Charles Darwin's son, specialize?

   A. Biology
   B. Anthropology
   C. Astronomy
   D. Paleontology

4. As of September 30, 1998, what percentage of Nevada land was owned by the U.S. government?

   A. 43
   B. 53
   C. 63
   D. 83

5. Which of the following is a name of an insect?

   A. Silverfish
   B. Daddy longlegs
   C. Scorpion
   D. Tick

6. Who was the first American commemorated by a monument constructed in India and unveiled in Bombay?

   A. George Washington Carver
   B. Franklin Roosevelt
   C. Abraham Lincoln
   D. Thomas Jefferson

7. Who was the first person ever to belch on national radio?

   A. Melvin Purvis
   B. Arthur Godfrey
   C. Bob Hope
   D. Franklin Delano Roosevelt

8. What is the real first name of ex-baseball player Whitey Ford?

   A. John
   B. James
   C. Raymond
   D. Edward

9. Who did *not* die in 1900?

   A. Friedrich Nietzsche
   B. Lewis Carroll
   C. Oscar Wilde
   D. Stephen Crane

10. What are persons who are interested in phillumeny interested in collecting?

    A. Postcards
    B. Matchbooks
    C. Subway tokens
    D. Beer coasters

11. What is the definition of *ucalegon*?

    A. A neighbor whose house is on fire
    B. An eleven-sided enclosed figure
    C. A beautiful woman
    D. A thick mist

12. What color is solferino?

A. Purplish red
B. Deep purple
C. Chestnut
D. Green with a bluish-gray tinge

13. In what year did Jack Nicklaus win his first golf tournament?

A. 1960
B. 1961
C. 1962
D. 1963

14. What is the state motto of Florida?

A. In God We Trust.
B. It is Perpetual.
C. Liberty and Prosperity.
D. Forever Young.

15. How many different personalities did the character of Sybil have in the TV movie *Sybil*?

A. 7
B. 9
C. 13
D. 16

ANSWERS ◆ TO $1,000,000 CHALLENGE #33

1. D. *Glenn Miller (for "Chattanooga Choo Choo")*
2. B. *Horace*
3. C. *Astronomy*
4. D. *83*
5. A. *Silverfish (The others are arachnids.)*
6. A. *George Washington Carver (in 1947)*
7. A. *Melvin Purvis (who was head of the Chicago office of the FBI and who burped during a 1935 broadcast)*
8. D. *Edward*
9. B. *Lewis Carroll (who died in 1898)*
10. B. *Matchbooks*
11. A. *A neighbor whose house is on fire*
12. A. *Purplish red*
13. C. *1962 (when he won the U.S. Open)*
14. A. *In God We Trust*
15. D. *16*

$1,000,000 CHALLENGE 34

1. What is a snath?

   A. A scythe handle
   B. A double-bladed handsaw
   C. A heart-shaped hoe
   D. A masonry tool used for finishing rough edges

2. What U.S. city is sometimes called the Candy Capital of the World?

   A. New York, New York
   B. Hershey, Pennsylvania
   C. Chicago, Illinois
   D. Camden, New Jersey

3. At the close of the year 2000, roughly in how many films had Jackie Chan, the Hong Kong actor, director, and producer, appeared?

   A. 40-plus
   B. 50-plus
   C. 60-plus
   D. 70-plus

4. Which of the following actors has won the most Emmys?

   A. Jerry Seinfeld
   B. Don Knotts
   C. Kelsey Grammer
   D. Drew Carey

5. Of the following films, which one received the most Oscar nominations?

   A. *All About Eve*
   B. *Rocky*
   C. *Gone With the Wind*
   D. *West Side Story*

6. What was the code name of Mrs. Roosevelt used during the Second World War?

A. Spot
B. Frisky
C. Sparky
D. Rover

7. Where was Francis Gary Powers going when his *U-2* plane was shot down over the Soviet Union in May 1960?

A. Norway
B. Sweden
C. Finland
D. Iceland

8. How many grooves are on the edge of a Roosevelt dime?

A. 109
B. 118
C. 119
D. 128

9. When was the title *Time*'s Man of the Year first conferred?

A. 1927
B. 1929
C. 1932
D. 1933

10. Which nation has been known as Portuguese West Africa?

A. Gabon
B. Nigeria
C. Angola
D. Guinea-Bissau

11. How many rooms are in the game of Clue?

A. 6
B. 7
C. 8
D. 9

12. Of what or whom is Cunina the Roman goddess?

A. Forests
B. Sleeping infants
C. Rising sun
D. Farmers

13. Where was the astronomer Tycho Brahe from?

A. Denmark
B. The Netherlands
C. France
D. Germany

14. Who is the patron goddess or muse of the game chess?

A. Melpomene
B. Adrastea
C. Caissa
D. Astraea

15. In music, what is the term for becoming *gradually* slower?

A. Allargando
B. Calando
C. Diminuendo
D. Rallentando

ANSWERS ◆ TO $1,000,000 CHALLENGE #34

1. A. *A scythe handle*
2. C. *Chicago, Illinois (home of Brachs and dozens of other candy companies. Hershey, Pennsylvania, is the Chocolate Capital of the World.)*
3. C. *60-plus*
4. B. *Don Knotts (who won the Best Actor Emmy five times for his role as Barney Fife)*
5. A. *All About Eve (14, the same number as Titanic)*
6. D. *Rover*
7. A. *Norway (Bodo)*
8. B. *118*
9. A. *1927 (on pilot Charles Lindberg)*
10. C. *Angola*
11. D. *9*
12. B. *Sleeping infants*
13. A. *Denmark*
14. C. *Caissa*
15. D. *Rallentando*

$1,000,000 CHALLENGE 35

1. Who engraved the plates for the first paper money issued by the Continental Congress?

   A. Alexander Hamilton **B.** Paul Revere
   C. Oliver Wolcott **D.** Albert Gallatin

2. Who was the first American to occupy what was called the position of Secretary of Defense?

   A. Robert Patterson **B.** Kenneth Royal
   C. James Forrestal **D.** Lewis Johnson

3. In what state did J. C. Penney open his first store?

   A. Oklahoma **B.** New Jersey
   C. Wyoming **D.** Illinois

4. How many siblings did William Shakespeare have?

   A. 4 **B.** 5
   C. 6 **D.** 7

5. Who was the first U.S. Secretary of War?

   A. Henry Knox **B.** Timothy Pickering
   C. James Moltenry **D.** Samuel Dexter

6. In *The Hobbit*, how many dwarfs escorted Bilbo Baggins from the Shire to the Lonely Mountains?

A. 7
B. 9
C. 11
D. 13

7. What did the father of Batman's Robin do for a living before he was killed?

A. Lawyer
B. Circus performer
C. Doctor
D. Professional athlete

8. To which signer of the Declaration of Independence is the actress Goldie Hawn directly related?

A. George Clymer
B. Edward Rutledge
C. Thomas Lynch, Jr.
D. Stephen Hopkins

9. To what cabinet department does the U.S. Weather Bureau belong?

A. Treasury
B. Commerce
C. Interior
D. Agriculture

10. In 2000, roughly what percentage of Americans were under 18?

A. 15
B. 20
C. 25
D. 30

11. According to a proclamation made by President Ronald Reagan on December 22, 1988, how far does the territorial sea of the U.S. extend from the shores of the country?

A. 3 nautical miles
B. 5 nautical miles
C. 12 nautical miles
D. 25 nautical miles

12. What two states were the end points of the first bridge to span the Mississippi River?

A. Missouri and Illinois | **B.** Minnesota and Wisconsin
C. Arkansas and Mississippi | **D.** Iowa and Illinois

13. In what year did the IBM computer Deep Blue defeat chess champion Garry Kasparov?

A. 1996 | **B.** 1997
C. 1998 | **D.** 1999

14. In 2001, what was the name of the world's fastest roller coaster?

A. Millennium Force | **B.** Fujiyama
C. Desperado | **D.** The Beast

15. What does the *C* stand for in J. C. Penney?

A. Carl | **B.** Charles
C. Cash | **D.** Carlton

ANSWERS ◆ TO $1,000,000 CHALLENGE #35

1. B. *Paul Revere*
2. C. *James Forrestal (Kenneth Royal was the last person to be called Secretary of War.)*
3. C. *Wyoming (in 1902)*
4. D. *7*
5. A. *Henry Knox*
6. D. *13*
7. B. *Circus performer (His parents were a high-wire act.)*
8. B. *Edward Rutledge*
9. B. *Commerce*
10. C. *25 (Officially, on July 1, 2000, 70 million U.S. residents [26 percent] were under 18.)*
11. C. *12 nautical miles*
12. D. *Iowa and Illinois*
13. B. *1997*
14. A. *Millennium Force (92 mph)*
15. C. *Cash*

$1,000,000 CHALLENGE 36

1. What was the name of General Grant's horse?

   A. Traveller
   B. Cincinnati
   C. Champion
   D. Morengo

2. A person who is discalced has no what?

   A. Hair
   B. Teeth
   C. Shoes
   D. Clothes

3. What was Fidel Castro wearing when Edward R. Morrow interviewed him on the TV show *Person to Person*?

   A. Military uniform
   B. Tuxedo
   C. Red pants and shirt
   D. Pajamas

4. What nation's capitol building is a replica of the U.S. Capitol, but on a smaller scale?

   A. Iceland's
   B. Mauritania's
   C. Java's
   D. Cuba's

5. Who wrote *Prometheus Bound*, including such characters as Io, Hermes, and Kratos?

   A. Aeschylus
   B. Shelley
   C. Milton
   D. Keats

6. What is the flavor of the Italian aperitif *punt e mes*?

A. Cherry | **B.** Orange
C. Coffee | **D.** Apple

7. An antithalian person will probably dislike what?

A. Parties | **B.** Wine
C. Religious gatherings | **D.** Physicians

8. What school is *not* one President Jimmy Carter attended?

A. U.S. Naval Academy | **B.** Georgia Southwestern College
C. Georgia Institute of Technology | **D.** Emory University

9. What does the name "Genghis Khan" literally mean?

A. Great One | **B.** Fearless One
C. Savior | **D.** Universal Ruler

10. What was the first bird to leave Noah's ark?

A. Dove | **B.** Raven
C. Owl | **D.** Eagle

11. For what newspaper did Janet Cooke work when she fabricated a story about "Jimmy," an 8-year-old heroin addict, which won a Pulitzer Prize and was later taken away?

A. *The New York Times* | **B.** *Washington Star*
C. *Washington Post* | **D.** *Atlanta Constitution*

12. What state did Vanessa Williams represent in the 1984 Miss America pageant?

    A. New York **B.** Indiana
    C. Michigan **D.** Georgia

13. So far as is currently known, which planet has the most moons?

    A. Saturn **B.** Jupiter
    C. Uranus **D.** Neptune

14. Shortly before he died, the philosopher, scientist, and mathematician Descartes tutored a queen from what country?

    A. France **B.** Germany
    C. Netherlands **D.** Sweden

15. Who directed the film *Midnight Express*?

    A. Mike Nichols **B.** John Schlesinger
    C. Alan Parker **D.** William Friedkin

ANSWERS ◆ TO $1,000,000 CHALLENGE #36

1. B. *Cincinnati*
2. C. *Shoes*
3. D. *Pajamas*
4. D. *Cuba*
5. A. *Aeschylus*
6. B. *Orange*
7. A. *Parties*
8. D. *Emory University*
9. D. *Universal Ruler*
10. B. *Raven*
11. C. Washington Post
12. A. *New York*
13. A. *Saturn*
14. D. *Sweden (Queen Christina)*
15. C. *Alan Parker*

$1,000,000 CHALLENGE 37

1. Who created the voice of the Little Penny puppet on the Penny Hardaway Nike ads?

   A. Adam Sandler | **B.** Jon Lovitz
   C. Chris Rock | **D.** Phil Hartman

2. Where was actress Minnie Driver born?

   A. England | **B.** Australia
   C. Barbados | **D.** St. Thomas (Virgin Islands)

3. To what confederacy do Mohawks belong?

   A. Iroquois | **B.** Apache
   C. Zuni | **D.** Seminole

4. With what country are the china-makers Minten and Royal Doulton associated?

   A. England | **B.** Ireland
   C. Scotland | **D.** Wales

5. What does epistemology study?

   A. Knowledge | **B.** Morality
   C. Reality | **D.** Beauty

6. What does an anemometer measure?

   A. Humidity
   B. Wind speed
   C. Barometric pressure
   D. Amount of precipitation

7. Tritium is a form of what?

   A. Uranium
   B. Oxygen
   C. Radium
   D. Hydrogen

8. Excluding future social security commitment, what was the national debt of the U.S. in the year 2000?

   A. $56 billion
   B. $560 billion
   C. $5.6 trillion
   D. $56 trillion

9. With what are event horizons associated?

   A. Solar eclipses
   B. Lunar eclipses
   C. Black holes
   D. Sun spots

10. What is the predominant religion of the Republic of the Ivory Coast?

    A. Islam
    B. Roman Catholicism
    C. Protestantism
    D. Hinduism

11. Who or what was the Pink Panther in the original 1964 movie of that name?

    A. Burglar
    B. Police detective
    C. Car
    D. Rare gem

12. How many U.S. gallons are in a barrel of oil?

A. 32 **B.** 42
C. 52 **D.** 62

13. What state contains mountains named Jackass, Tidbits, and Strawberry?

A. Oregon **B.** Washington
C. Montana **D.** Idaho

14. Who was the first senator in office to be elected president?

A. William Henry Harrison **B.** Benjamin Harrison
C. Warren Harding **D.** John Kennedy

15. Where is the College Football Hall of Fame?

A. Canton, Ohio **B.** Kings Island, Ohio
C. South Bend, Indiana **D.** Pasadena, California

ANSWERS ◆ TO $1,000,000 CHALLENGE #37

1. C. *Chris Rock*
2. C. *Barbados*
3. A. *Iroquois*
4. A. *England*
5. A. *Knowledge*
6. B. *Wind speed*
7. D. *Hydrogen*
8. C. *$5.6 trillion*
9. C. *Black holes*
10. A. *Islam*
11. D. *Rare gem*
12. B. *42*
13. A. *Oregon*
14. C. *Warren Harding*
15. C. *South Bend, Indiana (It used to be in Kings Island, Ohio.)*

$1,000,000 CHALLENGE 38

1. What was the name of Jerry Seinfeld's favorite snack food on *Seinfeld*?

A. Little Miss Debbie's Brownies **B.** Twinkies
C. Hostess Cupcakes **D.** Drake's Coffee Cake

2. What is the real name of rapper Ice-T?

A. Calvin Broadus **B.** O'Shea Jackson
C. Tracy Morrow **D.** Christopher Wallace

3. To what political party did President Millard Fillmore belong?

A. Whig **B.** Democrat
C. Republican **D.** Federalist

4. What does a nosologist study?

A. Noses **B.** Laws
C. Coins **D.** Diseases

5. What did British physicist James Chadwick discover?

A. Neutron **B.** Proton
C. Electron **D.** Quarks

6. What was the only number-one single by Peter, Paul, and Mary?

   A. "500 Miles"
   B. "Lemon Tree"
   C. "Blowin' in the Wind"
   D. "Leaving on a Jet Plane"

7. Who became the first golfer to win two different major tournaments in the 1990s?

   A. Tom Kite
   B. Payne Stewart
   C. Nick Faldo
   D. Fred Couples

8. If people are orgulous, they are what?

   A. Given to sexual indulgence
   B. Haughty
   C. Sinewy
   D. Unattractive

9. Near what coast will you find the Tortuga Islands?

   A. Florida
   B. California
   C. Argentina
   D. Western Australia

10. Who directed Michael Jackson in the 15-minute Epcot Center feature *Captain EO*?

    A. Francis Ford Coppola
    B. George Lucas
    C. Tim Robbins
    D. Steven Spielberg

11. When actor Chris O'Donnell took time off from pursuing a degree from Boston College to work with Al Pacino in *Scent of a Woman*, what was O'Donnell's principal area of study?

    A. English
    B. Broadcasting
    C. Drama
    D. Marketing

12. What size shoes does basketball player Shaquille O'Neal wear?

    A. 17 triple-E **B.** 19 triple-E
    C. 21 triple-E **D.** 23 triple-E

13. In what Woody Allen movie does Sylvester Stallone have a cameo appearance?

    A. *Bananas* **B.** *Sleeper*
    C. *Take the Money and Run* **D.** *Everything You Wanted to Know About Sex But Were Afraid to Ask*

14. Who said "As long as I can remember, I wanted to sleep late, stay up late, and do nothing in between"?

    A. Woody Allen **B.** Howard Stern
    C. Jon Stewart **D.** Craig Kilborn

15. Who nearly died in a car accident at 18, when his Fiat hit a car, flipped over, and crashed into a tree?

    A. Martin Scorsese **B.** Dennis Hopper
    C. Steven Seagal **D.** George Lucas

ANSWERS ◆ TO $1,000,000 CHALLENGE #38

1. D. *Drake's Coffee Cake*
2. C. *Tracy Morrow*
3. A. *Whig*
4. D. *Diseases (their classification)*
5. A. *Neutron*
6. D. *"Leaving on a Jet Plane"*
7. D. *Nick Faldo (who won the Masters in 1990 and the British Open in 1990 and 1992)*
8. B. *Haughty*
9. A. *Florida*
10. A. *Francis Ford Coppola*
11. D. *Marketing*
12. C. *21 triple-E*
13. A. Bananas
14. C. *Jon Stewart*
15. D. *George Lucas*

$1,000,000 CHALLENGE 39

1. What is a mudpuppy?

   A. Bug
   B. Bird
   C. Amphibian
   D. Fish

2. Who sought the worst jobs, including selling lightbulbs over the phone and costume jewelry on the streets, to force himself to succeed at comedy?

   A. Tim Conway
   B. Jerry Seinfeld
   C. Gary Shandling
   D. David Letterman

3. What comes in such varieties as monkey, short-horned, shield-backed, and pygmy?

   A. Grasshoppers
   B. Lizards
   C. Toads
   D. Salamanders

4. For which U.S. president was David Hume Kennerly the White House photographer?

   A. LBJ
   B. Nixon
   C. Ford
   D. Carter

5. Who decided to become a comic actress when she saw Jon Lovitz, her brother's childhood friend, make it on *Saturday Night Live*?

   A. Lisa Kudrow **B.** Calista Flockhart
   C. Julia Louis-Dreyfus **D.** Penny Marshall

6. On the TV series *The Jeffersons,* what was George Jefferson's main business competitor?

   A. Metro Cleaners **B.** Feldway Cleaners
   C. Albano Cleaners **D.** Sheckman Cleaners

7. Belleek is pottery resembling china and associated with what country?

   A. Netherlands **B.** Scotland
   C. Belgium **D.** Ireland

8. What is a group of turkeys?

   A. Rafter **B.** Gaggle
   C. Cluck **D.** Parcel

9. Something that is xanthic resembles what color?

   A. Blue **B.** Red
   C. Purple **D.** Yellow

10. The movie *Ordinary People* won all the following Academy Awards except:

    A. Best Picture **B.** Best Director
    C. Best Supporting Actor **D.** Best Actor

11. Where would someone find the Hagio Sophia Museum?

A. Berlin | **B.** Paris
C. Florence | **D.** Istanbul

12. In surveyors' measurement, how many links are in a chain?

A. 66 | **B.** 80
C. 100 | **D.** 144

13. Who, while working as a weather announcer at a local TV station, congratulated a tropical storm on being upgraded to a hurricane?

A. Jay Leno | **B.** David Letterman
C. Craig Kilborn | **D.** Johnny Carson

14. What is the smallest breed of tiger still extant?

A. Sumatran | **B.** Javan
C. Indian | **D.** Siberian

15. Which U.S. state has the second highest number of counties?

A. California | **B.** Kentucky
C. North Carolina | **D.** Georgia

ANSWERS ◆ TO $1,000,000 CHALLENGE #39

1. C. *Amphibian*
2. B. *Jerry Seinfeld*
3. A. *Grasshoppers*
4. C. *Ford*
5. A. *Lisa Kudrow*
6. B. *Feldway Cleaners*
7. D. *Ireland*
8. A. *Rafter*
9. D. *Yellow*
10. D. *Best Actor*
11. D. *Istanbul*
12. C. *100*
13. B. *David Letterman*
14. A. *Sumatran*
15. D. *Georgia (159)*

$1,000,000 CHALLENGE 40

1. According to Greek mythology, what material were the hands of the Gorgons made of?

   A. Brass
   B. Bronze
   C. Gold
   D. Copper

2. Roughly what percentage of your body is water?

   A. 62
   B. 70
   C. 75
   D. 82

3. How many gills of wine are in a hoggin?

   A. 5
   B. 4
   C. 2
   D. 1

4. Why was Kramer on *Seinfeld* banned from Joe's Fruit Market?

   A. He complained about a bad apple.
   B. He complained about a bad peach.
   C. He wouldn't stop belching.
   D. He insulted the owner.

5. In what constellation does the star Altair appear?

   A. Taurus
   B. Scorpius
   C. Orion
   D. Aquila

6. Where in the Bible does it read "The love of money is the root of all evil"?

   A. First Timothy
   B. Second Timothy
   C. First Corinthians
   D. Second Corinthians

7. What president used to like to quote the biblical verse "Come now, and let us reason together"?

   A. George Washington
   B. Calvin Coolidge
   C. Lyndon Johnson
   D. Jimmy Carter

8. What comes in such varieties as low, male, swamp, creeping, and late sweet?

   A. Raspberries
   B. Blackberries
   C. Blueberries
   D. Boysenberries

9. In the game of canasta, how many cards are in a hand?

   A. 5
   B. 7
   C. 10
   D. 11

10. What Shakespearean play was quoted from at the end of the Beatles' "I Am the Walrus"?

    A. *King Lear*
    B. *Macbeth*
    C. *Hamlet*
    D. *Richard III*

11. Which of the following presidents studied to become a medical doctor?

    A. William Henry Harrison
    B. Millard Fillmore
    C. Franklin Pierce
    D. Rutherford B. Hayes

12. Who once wrote for *Mad* magazine?

A. Gilda Radner | **B.** Dan Aykroyd
C. Chevy Chase | **D.** Jane Curtain

13. How old was Sleeping Beauty when she fell into a deep sleep, according to the Disney movie?

A. 14 | **B.** 15
C. 16 | **D.** 18

14. Where did author Joseph Wambaugh first learn to be a police officer?

A. New York | **B.** Chicago
C. Detroit | **D.** Los Angeles

15. Who was the first American president officially to receive a female ambassador?

A. H. Hoover | **B.** F. Roosevelt
C. Eisenhower | **D.** Truman

ANSWERS ◆ TO $1,000,000 CHALLENGE #40

1. A. *Brass*
2. A. *62*
3. D. *I*
4. B. *He complained about a bad peach.*
5. D. *Aquila*
6. A. *First Timothy*
7. C. *Lyndon Johnson*
8. C. *Blueberries*
9. D. *11*
10. A. King Lear
11. A. *William Henry Harrison*
12. C. *Chevy Chase*
13. C. *16*
14. D. *Los Angeles*
15. D. *Truman*

$1,000,000 CHALLENGE 41

1. Where was Mark Twain born?

   A. Hannibal, Missouri
   B. Independence, Missouri
   C. Joplin, Missouri
   D. Florida, Missouri

2. Who was the architect of the Harvard University Graduate Center?

   A. I. M. Pei
   B. Ludwig Mies van der Robe
   C. Walter Gropius
   D. Louis Sullivan

3. What is the highest honor a children's picture book can receive?

   A. Newbery Medal
   B. Hans Christian Andersen Award
   C. Caldecott Medal
   D. Dr. Seuss Award

4. What animal is different from the other three (which are different names for the same animal)?

   A. Mountain Lion
   B. Jaguar
   C. Cougar
   D. Puma

5. What U.S. general referred to his advance headquarters as Lucky Forward?

   A. George S. Patton
   B. Dwight D. Eisenhower
   C. Joseph Stilwell
   D. Douglas MacArthur

6. What country's flag is entirely red except for a star in its center?

   A. Samoa
   B. Morocco
   C. Myanmar (Burma)
   D. Tonga

7. In 1990, about how many Americans were at least 100 years old?

   A. 15,000
   B. 25,000
   C. 36,000
   D. 41,000

8. In 1998, which state received the second highest number of immigrants?

   A. New York
   B. Florida
   C. Texas
   D. New Jersey

9. Which country's flag is not rectangular but slightly resembles the profile of a bird?

   A. Nauru
   B. Nepal
   C. Mauritania
   D. Lesotho

10. Musicians are not eligible for the Rock and Roll Hall of Fame until how many years after their first record?

    A. 20
    B. 24
    C. 25
    D. 30

11. Where is the National Cowboy Hall of Fame and Western Heritage Center?

    A. Dallas, Texas
    B. San Antonio, Texas
    C. Abilene, Kansas
    D. Oklahoma City, Oklahoma

12. About how much was the U.S. federal budget deficit in 1997?

A. $23 billion
B. $107 billion
C. $164 billion
D. $203 billion

13. What was the first name of the father of *Star Trek*'s Captain James Kirk?

A. Robert
B. Peter
C. Richard
D. James

14. Where are the Freer Gallery of Art and Arthur M. Sackler Gallery?

A. Washington, D.C.
B. New York, New York
C. Los Angeles, California
D. Phoenix, Arizona

15. In the 1999 budget year, what percentage of the U.S. federal budget was allocated for interest on the national debt?

A. 15
B. 21
C. 18
D. 25

ANSWERS ◆ **TO $1,000,000 CHALLENGE #41**

1. D. *Florida, Missouri*
2. C. *Walter Gropius*
3. C. *Caldecott Award*
4. B. *Jaguar*
5. A. *George S. Patton*
6. B. *Morocco*
7. C. *36,000*
8. A. *New York*
9. B. *Nepal*
10. C. *25*
11. D. *Oklahoma City, Oklahoma*
12. A. *$23 billion*
13. B. *Peter*
14. A. *Washington, D.C.*
15. B. *21*

$1,000,000 CHALLENGE 42

1. How many gallons of beer are in a U.S. anker?

   A. 2 **B.** 6
   C. 8 **D.** 10

2. Whose last movie was called *The Killers*?

   A. Cary Grant **B.** Humphrey Bogart
   C. Ronald Reagan **D.** George Raft

3. What is a baby beaver called?

   A. Calf **B.** Kitten
   C. Pup **D.** Baby

4. What is a group of boars called?

   A. Pack **B.** Sounder
   C. Team **D.** Clamor

5. In the 1950 U.S. census, what basketball player's great-grandfather was declared the oldest living person in the U.S. (age 116)?

   A. Walt Frazier **B.** Willis Reed
   C. Jerry West **D.** Oscar Robertson

6. How many ounces did Babe Ruth's bat, Black Bess, weigh?

A. 38 **B.** 40
C. 42 **D.** 44

7. What state contains Meadville, State College, and Mill Creek?

A. Ohio **B.** Indiana
C. Illinois **D.** Pennsylvania

8. Which argument for the existence of God does *not* assume the existence of the physical world or people?

A. Argument from design **B.** Argument from a first cause
C. Ontological argument **D.** Pascal's Wager

9. Where is Canoe City?

A. Florida **B.** California
C. Maine **D.** Washington

10. Of what U.S. military service is Hap Arnold the father?

A. Air Force **B.** Coast Guard
C. Marines **D.** Navy

11. Who is sometimes called the First American Man of Letters?

A. Benjamin Franklin **B.** Washington Irving
C. Ralph Waldo Emerson **D.** Mark Twain

12. Who said "It is a sin to be born"?

A. Nietzsche
B. Diogenes
C. Schopenhauer
D. Oscar Wilde

13. What was the first name of Mr. Shrapnel, the English artillery officer who invented shrapnel?

A. Henry
B. Thomas
C. Richard
D. Winston

14. What was the name of Adolf Hitler's dog?

A. Hans
B. Klaus
C. Max
D. Blondi

15. What was the name of Charlie Brown's elementary school?

A. Birchwood Elementary
B. Grant Avenue Elementary
C. Pinewood Elementary
D. Oak Avenue Elementary

ANSWERS ◆ TO $1,000,000 CHALLENGE #42

1. **D.** *10*
2. **C.** *Ronald Reagan*
3. **B.** *Kitten*
4. **B.** *Sounder*
5. **D.** *Oscar Robertson*
6. **D.** *44*
7. **D.** *Pennsylvania*
8. **C.** *Ontological argument*
9. **C.** *Maine (Old Town)*
10. **A.** *Air Force*
11. **B.** *Washington Irving*
12. **C.** *Schopenhauer*
13. **A.** *Henry*
14. **D.** *Blondi*
15. **A.** *Birchwood Elementary*

$1,000,000 CHALLENGE 43

1. What rap musician recorded the albums *Death Certificate* and *Lethal Injection*?

   A. LL Cool J
   B. Snoop Doggy Dogg
   C. Dr. Dre
   D. Ice Cube

2. What Old Testament prophet was teased by a group of children because he was bald?

   A. Elijah
   B. Elisha
   C. Ezekiel
   D. Micah

3. In mythology, who was Prometheus's father?

   A. Iapetus
   B. Atlas
   C. Deucalion
   D. Zeus

4. Which is *not* a satellite of Saturn?

   A. Titan
   B. Janus
   C. Callisto
   D. Hyperion

5. What does the name of the constellation Dorado mean?

   A. Goldfish
   B. Dolphin
   C. Dragon
   D. Dove

6. What role did William Shakespeare play when he appeared in the production of *Hamlet*?

   A. Claudius
   B. The ghost/spirit of Hamlet's father
   C. Laertes
   D. Hamlet

7. Who received Medicare Card No. 1?

   A. Dwight Eisenhower
   B. Richard Nixon
   C. Harry Truman
   D. Lyndon Johnson

8. Where was Jack Dempsey from?

   A. California
   B. Colorado
   C. Ohio
   D. Arizona

9. What was the nickname of the historical person on whom the cinematic character of Minnesota Fats was based?

   A. New York Fats
   B. Ohio Fats
   C. New Jersey Fats
   D. California Fats

10. Who is the only non-music performer to win the Grammy for Best New Artist?

   A. Bob Newhart
   B. Woody Allen
   C. George Carlin
   D. Shelley Berman

11. What is a linden?

   A. Tree
   B. Plant
   C. Animal
   D. Dwelling

12. What president used to tell reporters "Let me just say this about that"?

A. Truman | **B.** Eisenhower
C. Nixon | **D.** Ford

13. Which Marx brother died first?

A. Chico | **B.** Harpo
C. Groucho | **D.** Gummo

14. For what soft drink company was Richard Nixon once a lawyer?

A. Pepsi-Cola | **B.** Coca-Cola
C. Dr Pepper | **D.** Royal Crown

15. How much would a 420-pound man weigh on the moon?

A. 140 lbs. | **B.** 105 lbs.
C. 60 lbs. | **D.** 70 lbs.

ANSWERS ◆ TO $1,000,000 CHALLENGE #43

1. D. *Ice Cube*
2. B. *Elisha*
3. A. *Iapetus*
4. C. *Callisto (a moon of Jupiter)*
5. A. *Goldfish*
6. B. *The ghost/spirit of Hamlet's father*
7. C. *Harry Truman*
8. B. *Colorado*
9. A. *New York Fats*
10. A. *Bob Newhart (for his 1960 LP Button-Down Mind, which also won Grammys for Album of the Year and Best Comedy Performance)*
11. A. *Tree*
12. C. *Nixon*
13. A. *Chico*
14. A. *Pepsi-Cola*
15. D. *70 lbs. (because the gravitational pull on the surface of the moon is about one-sixth as strong as it is on Earth)*

$1,000,000 CHALLENGE 44

1. How deep is a twain?

   A. 6 feet
   B. 10 feet
   C. 12 feet
   D. 14 feet

2. What was the original nickname of fighter plane F101?

   A. Super Sabre
   B. Voodoo
   C. Delta Dagger
   D. Starfighter

3. Who played the Tin Man in the 1925 silent movie version of *The Wizard of Oz*?

   A. Douglas Fairbanks
   B. Ronald Colman
   C. Bud Abbott
   D. Oliver Hardy

4. In Greek mythology, who was the mother of the Gorgons?

   A. Dirae
   B. Semnai
   C. Ceto
   D. Megaera

5. What is a group of gorillas called?

   A. Club
   B. Tribe
   C. Crash
   D. Band

6. What is the name of a drink containing gin and sherry?

A. Bloodhound
B. Renaissance
C. Abbey
D. Red Lion

7. What university did Bill Mahr attend?

A. Harvard
B. Princeton
C. Cornell
D. Yale

8. To what actor did Greta Garbo say "I want to be alone"?

A. John Barrymore
B. Lionel Barrymore
C. Wallace Beery
D. Lewis Stone

9. During what month was the Boston Tea Party?

A. April
B. July
C. October
D. December

10. Who once had a job answering mail for cartoon characters Tom and Jerry?

A. Robert Duvall
B. Al Pacino
C. Jack Nicholson
D. Gene Hackman

11. What is the last year in which the Buffalo nickel was minted?

A. 1935
B. 1937
C. 1936
D. 1938

12. What is the name of the first American president with an MBA degree?

A. W. Harding **B.** C. Coolidge
C. H. Hoover **D.** G.W. Bush

13. After leaving the White House but before serving in the U.S. Supreme Court, where did William Howard Taft teach constitutional law?

A. Yale **B.** Harvard
C. Columbia **D.** Georgetown

14. How many U.S. senators voted against the 1964 Gulf of Tonkin resolution authorizing U.S. involvement in Vietnam?

A. 0 **B.** 1
C. 2 **D.** 4

15. Who was the only performer to appear on TV's *American Bandstand* performing live rather than lip-synching?

A. Roy Orbison **B.** Johnny Cash
C. Tom Jones **D.** B. B. King

ANSWERS ◆ TO $1,000,000 CHALLENGE #44

1. C. *12 feet (2 fathoms)*
2. B. *Voodoo*
3. D. *Oliver Hardy*
4. C. *Ceto*
5. D. *Band*
6. B. *Renaissance*
7. C. *Cornell*
8. A. *John Barrymore* (in Grand Hotel)
9. D. *December* (specifically, December 16, 1773)
10. C. *Jack Nicholson*
11. D. *1938*
12. D. *G.W. Bush*
13. A. *Yale*
14. C. *2*
15. D. *B.B. King*

$1,000,000 CHALLENGE 45

1. How many members are on a hurling team?

   A. 9 **B.** 10
   C. 11 **D.** 15

2. What is the name given to the North Korean pilot who flies a sputtering plane while unsuccessfully trying to bomb the 4077th MASH unit in the TV show *M*A*S*H*?

   A. 2 O'Clock Charlie **B.** 3 O'Clock Charlie
   C. 4 O'Clock Charlie **D.** 5 O'Clock Charlie

3. How many of the original members of the Justice League of America were there?

   A. 5 **B.** 6
   C. 7 **D.** 8

4. Which one of the following schools is private rather than public?

   A. University of Pennsylvania **B.** University of Virginia
   C. University of Michigan **D.** College of William and Mary

5. Who received card No. 1 of TVA, the first television actors' union?

   A. Art Linkletter **B.** Bob Keeshan
   C. Steve Allen **D.** Arthur Godfrey

6. Who was *not* one of the five little peppers in the novel *Five Little Peppers and How They Grew*?

A. Ben | **B.** Polly
C. Jimmy | **D.** Joel

7. For what newspaper did Tim O'Hara work in the TV series *My Favorite Martian*?

A. *The Los Angeles Herald* | **B.** *The Los Angeles Bugle*
C. *The Los Angeles Gazette* | **D.** *The Los Angeles Sun*

8. Who played "The Missouri Waltz" for Harry Truman in Independence, Missouri, on March 21, 1969?

A. Richard Nixon | **B.** Lyndon Johnson
C. Dwight Eisenhower | **D.** Steve Allen

9. What was the first daytime soap opera to expand to one hour?

A. *Another World* | **B.** *As the World Turns*
C. *The Edge of Night* | **D.** *General Hospital*

10. Who finished right behind Richard Nixon in delegate votes in the 1968 Republican National Convention?

A. Barry Goldwater | **B.** Nelson Rockefeller
C. Ronald Reagan | **D.** Henry Cabot Lodge

11. Which country has a flag containing no yellow?

A. Tanzania | **B.** Vietnam
C. Venezuela | **D.** Nigeria

12. Which president appointed at least one justice to the U.S. Supreme Court?

A. William H. Harrison
B. Zachary Taylor
C. John F. Kennedy
D. Jimmy Carter

13. What soft drink was originally known as Brad's drink?

A. Coca-Cola
B. Dr Pepper
C. 7 Up
D. Pepsi

14. According to *The Essential Bond: The Authorized Guide to the World of 007,* whom did Ian Fleming initially ask to play the part of Dr. No?

A. Noel Coward
B. Patrick McGoohan
C. Roger Moore
D. Christopher Lee

15. What was the only product for which Elvis Presley made a TV commercial?

A. Cars
B. Doughnuts
C. Guitars
D. Hair cream

ANSWERS ♦ TO $1,000,000 CHALLENGE #45

1. D. *15*
2. D. *5 O'Clock Charlie*
3. C. *7*
4. A. *University of Pennsylvania*
5. B. *Bob Keeshan (Captain Kangaroo)*
6. C. *Jimmy (The others are Davie and Phronsie.)*
7. D. The Los Angeles Sun
8. A. *Richard Nixon*
9. A. Another World
10. B. *Nelson Rockefeller*
11. D. *Nigeria*
12. C. *John F. Kennedy*
13. D. *Pepsi*
14. A. *Noel Coward*
15. B. *Doughnuts*

$1,000,000 CHALLENGE 46

1. What was the last name of the inventor of Coca-Cola?

   A. Lazenby **B.** Cronan
   C. Pemberton **D.** Paulson

2. Sydney is the capital of what division in Australia?

   A. Queensland **B.** South Australia
   C. Northern Territory **D.** New South Wales

3. Who originally said "Those who restrain desire do so because theirs is weak enough to be restrained . . ."?

   A. Oscar Wilde **B.** Walter Pater
   C. Henry Miller **D.** William Blake

4. Who wrote "My own mind is my own church"?

   A. Thomas Paine **B.** Thomas Jefferson
   C. Martin Luther **D.** Bertrand Russell

5. What was the "real identity" of Captain America?

   A. Billy Batson **B.** Peter Parker
   C. Hal Jordan **D.** Steve Rogers

6. Who was the only player to hit a home run in the 1919 World Series?

   A. Joe Jackson
   B. Chick Gandil
   C. Buck Weaver
   D. Swede Risberg

7. What is the motto of the Salvation Army (displayed on their emblem)?

   A. Faith and Love
   B. Blood and Fire
   C. Charity and Love
   D. Love and Fire

8. What was the name of the motorcycle gang in the 1954 movie *The Wild One*?

   A. The Scorpions
   B. The Roughriders
   C. Black Rebels
   D. The Wild Ones

9. Who created the character of Dick Tracy?

   A. Mickey Spillane
   B. Jack Perl
   C. Donald Hamilton
   D. Chester Gould

10. All the Four Horsemen of Notre Dame usually weighed less than what?

    A. 170 pounds
    B. 180 pounds
    C. 190 pounds
    D. 200 pounds

11. What Indian tribe is *not* a member of The Five Nations or the Iroquois League?

    A. Seneca
    B. Mohawk
    C. Cheyenne
    D. Oneida

12. Which one of the following ships was sunk at Pearl Harbor?

A. *Oklahoma* **B.** *Pennsylvania*
C. *Tennessee* **D.** *Maryland*

13. Where was the Alaskan gold discovery in 1886?

A. Thirtymile Creek **B.** Fortymile Creek
C. Fiftymile Creek **D.** Sixtymile Creek

14. Something that is dolioform is shaped like a what?

A. Barrel **B.** Worm
C. Key hole **D.** Hourglass

15. What does a sazerac cocktail *not* contain?

A. Bourbon **B.** Bitters
C. Absinthe **D.** Orange juice

ANSWERS ◆ TO $1,000,000 CHALLENGE #46

1. C. *Pemberton*
2. D. *New South Wales*
3. D. *William Blake*
4. A. *Thomas Paine*
5. D. *Steve Rogers*
6. A. *Joe Jackson*
7. B. *Blood and Fire*
8. C. *Black Rebels*
9. D. *Chester Gould*
10. A. *170 pounds*
11. C. *Cheyenne (The other two are the Cayuga and the Onondaga.)*
12. A. Oklahoma
13. B. *Fortymile Creek*
14. A. *Barrel*
15. D. *Orange juice*

$1,000,000 CHALLENGE 47

1. In the comics, what is the name of Jughead's cousin who strongly resembles him?

   A. Souphead　　**B.** Meathead
   C. Lughead　　**D.** Vacuumhead

2. The first federal highway (Cumberland Road) went from Cumberland, Maryland, to where in Illinois?

   A. Bloomington　　**B.** Joliet
   C. Evanston　　**D.** Vandalia

3. What pianist sold a million records in 1962 of *Tchaikovsky's First Piano Concerto*?

   A. Van Cliburn　　**B.** A. Rubinstein
   C. Liberace　　**D.** V. Horowitz

4. Whose original name was Leonard Slye?

   A. Roy Clark　　**B.** Roy Rogers
   C. Danny Thomas　　**D.** Richard Kiley

5. Where did the dolls Barbie and Ken attend high school?

   A. Pinewood High School　　**B.** Pinewell High School
   C. Willows High School　　**D.** Oakdale High School

6. What boxer was nicknamed the Mongoose?

A. Jersey Joe Walcott
B. Archie Moore
C. Sonny Liston
D. Ezzard Charles

7. Which Beatle lived at 174 Mackets Lane, Liverpool?

A. Paul McCartney
B. John Lennon
C. George Harrison
D. Ringo Star

8. Which Bob Dylan song was inspired by the blues song "No More Auction Block for Me"?

A. "Blowin' in the Wind"
B. "Times They Are A-Changin' "
C. "Like a Rolling Stone"
D. "Mr. Tambourine Man"

9. Whom did James Dean beat out for the lead role in the movie *East of Eden*?

A. Marlon Brando
B. Warren Beatty
C. Robert Wagner
D. Paul Newman

10. Which Beatle said "We can't sing. We can't do anything. We're just having a good time"?

A. John Lennon
B. Paul McCartney
C. Ringo Star
D. George Harrison

11. What planet did *Pioneer II* take a close look at on September 1, 1979?

A. Mars
B. Jupiter
C. Saturn
D. Uranus

12. What was the first hit of the music group The Four Seasons?

A. "Sherry" **B.** "Rag Doll"
C. "Walk Like a Man" **D.** "Big Girls Don't Cry"

13. Which Beach Boy hit was inspired by Chuck Berry's "Sweet Little Sixteen"?

A. "Surfin' U.S.A." **B.** "I Get Around"
C. "Barbara Ann" **D.** "Help Me Rhonda"

14. What color of paper was the fifty-cents currency issued by the Confederate States of America?

A. Pink **B.** Yellow
C. Green **D.** Blue

15. Where in Europe will you find a sculpture of a giant paper clip?

A. Stockholm, Sweden **B.** Oslo, Norway
C. Paris, France **D.** Brussels, Belgium

ANSWERS ◆ TO $1,000,000 CHALLENGE #47

1. A. *Souphead*
2. D. *Vandalia*
3. A. *Van Cliburn*
4. B. *Roy Rogers*
5. C. *Willows High School*
6. B. *Archie Moore*
7. C. *George Harrison*
8. A. *"Blowin' in the Wind"*
9. D. *Paul Newman*
10. B. *Paul McCartney*
11. C. *Saturn*
12. A. *"Sherry"*
13. A. *"Surfin' U.S.A."*
14. A. *Pink (with Jefferson Davis's picture)*
15. B. *Oslo, Norway (home of the inventor of the paper clip, Johann Vaaler)*

$1,000,000 CHALLENGE 48

1. What was the name of Dick Tracy's textbook of crime fighting?

   A. *Crimestoppers* **B.** *Crimefighting*
   C. *Forensics* **D.** *Criminology*

2. What was the name of Sir Isaac Newton's spaniel?

   A. Diamond **B.** Cerebus
   C. Odysseus **D.** Jupiter

3. What is the name of the little kitten on the logo of TV's Mary Tyler Moore productions?

   A. Tabby Marino **B.** Tony Martin
   C. Tabby Martin **D.** Dick Marino

4. Where is Devil's Tower, America's first national monument?

   A. North Dakota **B.** South Dakota
   C. Wyoming **D.** Montana

5. Who played a prisoner called Dragline in *Cool Hand Luke*?

   A. George Kennedy **B.** Wayne Rogers
   C. Anthony Zerbe **D.** Dennis Hopper

6. What is the name of Dudley Do-Right's horse?

A. Pegasus
B. Horse
C. Whinny
D. Dog

7. In the music duet of Jan and Dean, what is Dean's last name?

A. Berry
B. Prater
C. Paxton
D. Torrence

8. What actor was once the public address announcer at Ebbets Field, home of the Brooklyn Dodgers?

A. John Forsythe
B. Joseph Cotton
C. Douglas Fairbanks, Jr.
D. Stuart Whitman

9. In what school did Wally Cox and Marlon Brando attend the same fourth-grade class?

A. Rockford Elementary
B. Bloomington Elementary
C. Evanston Elementary
D. Decator Elementary

10. How many hats were worn by Dr. Seuss's Bartholomew Cubbins?

A. 200
B. 300
C. 400
D. 500

11. In the TV show *Banacek*, what was Banacek's first name?

A. Robert
B. Thomas
C. James
D. Richard

12. Who was the voice of Matt Dillon on the radio show *Gunsmoke*?

A. William Conrad
B. Gene Barry
C. Glenn Ford
D. Jack Palance

13. Who was nicknamed the First Lady of the Screen?

A. Clara Bow
B. Helen Hayes
C. Norma Shearer
D. Norma Talmadge

14. What gun did the character Alexander Scott use in the TV show *I Spy*?

A. .357 Magnum
B. .38 automatic
C. Luger Special "S"
D. .32 Police

15. What baseball pitcher was nicknamed the Big Train?

A. Walter Johnson
B. Bob Gibson
C. Don Drysdale
D. Bob Feller

ANSWERS ◆ TO $1,000,000 CHALLENGE #48

1. A. Crimestoppers (*shown on the first panel of a Dick Tracy comic strip*)
2. A. *Diamond*
3. D. *Dick Marino*
4. C. *Wyoming*
5. A. *George Kennedy*
6. B. *Horse*
7. D. *Torrence*
8. A. *John Forsythe*
9. C. *Evanston Elementary*
10. D. *500*
11. B. *Thomas*
12. A. *William Conrad*
13. C. *Norma Shearer*
14. A. *.357 Magnum*
15. A. *Walter Johnson*

$1,000,000 CHALLENGE 49

1. Which of the following is an acaleph?

   A. Tropical tree **B.** Jellyfish
   C. Religious official **D.** Fraternity

2. What was James Dean's real last name?

   A. Byron **B.** Richards
   C. Burns **D.** Keats

3. Which is not a moon of Jupiter?

   A. Ganymede **B.** Callisto
   C. Phobos **D.** Europa

4. In India's caste system, who are the workers?

   A. Vaisyas **B.** Kshatriyas
   C. Brahmans **D.** Sudras

5. How fast is the wind in a gale warning, according to Small-Craft Advisory alerts issued by the National Weather Service?

   A. 16–32 knots **B.** 32–34 knots
   C. 34–47 knots **D.** 47–63 knots

6. In Japanese hierarchy, which of the following is a department manager?

A. Kaicho
B. Shacho
C. Bucho
D. Kacho

7. Where was the first colony to legalize slavery?

A. Connecticut
B. Massachusetts
C. Virginia
D. Delaware

8. What does *scansorial* mean?

A. Adapted for climbing
B. Adapted for walking
C. Adapted for grasping
D. Adapted for jumping

9. Which boxer held three world titles at the same time?

A. Harry Greb
B. Stanley Ketchel
C. Sugar Ray Robinson
D. Henry Armstrong

10. What is a boletus?

A. Soup
B. Sweet bread
C. Mushroom
D. Green vegetable

11. What discipline deals with questions of values?

A. Axiology
B. Ontology
C. Soteriology
D. Epistemology

12. What was the first toy advertised on TV?

A. Slinky
B. Silly Putty
C. Play-Doh
D. Mr. Potato Head

13. Which person appeared on both TV's *$64,000 Question* and *The $64,000 Challenge*?

A. Robert Preston
B. Dr. Joyce Brothers
C. Vincent Price
D. Edward G. Robinson

14. Who originally hosted the TV show *Twenty-One*?

A. Jack Barry
B. Hal March
C. Ralph Story
D. Ralph Edwards

15. Who was the first American president to ride to his inauguration in an automobile?

A. T. Roosevelt
B. Wilson
C. Harding
D. Coolidge

ANSWERS ◆ TO $1,000,000 CHALLENGE #49

1. B. *Jellyfish*
2. A. *Byron*
3. C. *Phobos (a Martian moon)*
4. D. *Sudras*
5. C. *34–47 knots*
6. C. *Bucho*
7. B. *Massachusetts (in 1641)*
8. A. *Adapted for climbing*
9. D. *Henry Armstrong*
10. C. *Mushroom*
11. A. *Axiology*
12. D. *Mr. Potato Head*
13. B. *Dr. Joyce Brothers*
14. A. *Jack Barry*
15. C. *Harding*

$1,000,000 CHALLENGE 50

1. Where is General Douglas MacArthur buried?

A. Arlington, Virginia
B. West Point, New York
C. Washington, D.C.
D. Norfolk, Virginia

2. With what thing is the god Janus *not* associated?

A. Moon
B. Rising sun
C. Doorways
D. Setting sun

3. Who was *not* a son of Jason the Argonaut?

A. Pheres
B. Pelias
C. Medelus
D. Mermerus

4. Who was the first American president to major in history and government at college?

A. William Howard Taft
B. Theodore Roosevelt
C. Woodrow Wilson
D. James Garfield

5. What was the name of the Brady family's pet dog on the TV cartoon series *The Brady Kids*?

A. Moptop
B. Tramp
C. Tiger
D. Pooch

6. In what two years did the same person win the Olympic decathlon?

A. 1948, 1952
B. 1956, 1960
C. 1964, 1968
D. 1968, 1972

7. What was the name of Beep Beep, the Road Runner's wife?

A. Bertha
B. Matilda
C. Charlotte
D. Gertrude

8. In what branch of service did detective Matt Helm serve?

A. Army
B. Air Force
C. Marines
D. Navy

9. Where was Philadelphia brand cream cheese introduced?

A. New York
B. Chicago
C. Detroit
D. Boston

10. What actor was nicknamed the Great Profile?

A. Douglas Fairbanks, Sr.
B. John Barrymore
C. Cary Grant
D. Errol Flynn

11. Where was actress Joan Fontaine born?

A. England
B. Canada
C. Japan
D. Ireland

12. What is the only U.S. state without caves?

A. Hawaii
B. Florida
C. Rhode Island
D. Delaware

13. What did William Lear invent besides the Learjet?

A. Audio cassette recorder
B. 8-track stereo
C. Electronic calculator
D. Video games

14. Of the following states, which did not approve of Prohibition?

A. New York
B. Georgia
C. Massachusetts
D. Rhode Island

15. What is the name of Caractacus Potts's shaggy pet dog in the 1968 movie *Chitty Chitty Bang Bang*?

A. Edison
B. Einstein
C. Emerson
D. Newton

ANSWERS ◆ TO $1,000,000 CHALLENGE #50

1. D. *Norfolk, Virginia*
2. A. *Moon*
3. B. *Pelias (his half-brother)*
4. C. *Woodrow Wilson*
5. A. *Moptop*
6. A. *1948, 1952*
7. B. *Matilda*
8. D. *Navy*
9. A. *New York*
10. B. *John Barrymore*
11. C. *Japan*
12. C. *Rhode Island*
13. B. *8-track stereo*
14. D. *Rhode Island*
15. A. *Edison*

John Carpenter is a Rutgers graduate who majored in economics. As a contestant on television's *Who Wants to Be a Millionaire,* he became the first person in history to win one million dollars on a game show. Known by friends for his wide range of knowledge, Carpenter finishes the *New York Times* crossword puzzle every day at lunch.

Rod L. Evans, Ph.D., is the author of several books on interpersonal communications, including *Weird Words, More Weird Words, The Dictionary of Highly Unusual Words, Getting Your Words' Worth,* and *The Right Words.* Evans teaches philosophy at Old Dominion University in Norfolk, Virginia.